Dear Elephant, Sir

DEAR ELEPHANT, SIR

CLIVE WALKER

Edited by Sally Antrobus

Illustrations by Clive Walker

SOUTHERN
BOOK PUBLISHERS

Dedication

Some twenty years ago, Romain Gary wrote a letter to an elephant in an issue of a Time-Life magazine, clearly signalling a warning about the fate that could befall these giants. Little did we know just how right he was. The letter, "Dear Elephant, Sir . . ." had a profound effect upon me at the time and I resolved to write a book one day about my own experiences with elephants. The text, drawings, and photographs here represent that attempt to record my sentiments and, I would like to believe, those of Romain Gary. In near conclusion to his letter, he wrote: "In a truly materialistic and realistic society, poets, writers, artists, dreamers and elephants are a mere nuisance."

This book is therefore humbly dedicated to poets, writers, artists, dreamers and elephants.

Contents

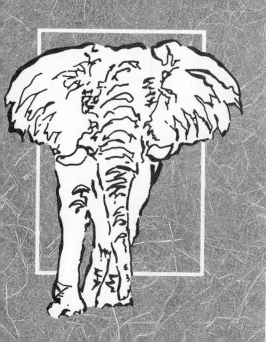

*My Dad killed a big elephant
and he killed a big lion
and other things*

*Michelle Rod
Houston, Texas*

(Safari company visitor book
Maun, Botswana)

Foreword

When Romain Gary's prescient tribute to the African elephant was first published I was living in a mud hut in the Kasungu National Park, in what was then a fairly remote corner of Malawi. It made a deep and abiding impression on me and I still have my copy of that special issue of Life magazine. Now, all these years later, I am intrigued to find that Clive Walker read the same issue of Life – I recall it had a Peter Beard photograph of a mud-covered Tsavo elephant bull on the cover. Elephants were dominating theme of my life at the time, they still are now. For Clive Walker it was equally so. It was not too long after my return to South Africa that I began to take note of the man who in 1973 first went public with his print appeals for endangered wild animals – including the magnificent African elephant – when such overt public commitment to conservation issues was new and daring.

We met formally when I was doing research on the Addo elephants and Clive offered financial support for some of my work. Since then we have collaborated on field projects, several books and on expeditions to some of the wilder and most beautiful corners of Africa. We have made numerous visits to the Kaokoveld, Tuli, Savuti and Chobe; Augrabies and Vaalbos; Sihangwane, the Kruger National Park, Zimbabwe and Kenya. On many of these trips, to study elephants and black rhinoceros, we have been accompanied by close friends, in particular Peter Hitchins and Lloyd Wilmot, and the process of being immersed in elephant and ivory issues has been the counterpoint of our long and warm friendship. There have been many milestones in Clive Walker's career that hinged on elephant issues, and I have been fortunate to share a number of them with him.

The importance of elephants and the heated
issues evoked by elephant management and conservation, have been *leit motif* of Clive Walker's
life and work. This comes out strongly in these
fascinating essays which not only highlight the
elephant, but also show Clive's concern for wider
environmental and conservation issues. Clive has
been a pioneer in South African conservation circles, in fund raising, in field projects and in pub-
licising the issues. His many talents as writer,
artist, teacher, photographer and public speaker
have all been employed to the greater good of
wildlife and wild places in general, and rhinos
and elephants in particular.

It is a measure of this sincere and talented man
that his work has imbued and inspired so many
other people to take note of the wild, to enjoy it
and to care for it. If Clive Walker feels any shame
for that first elephant he killed he can be assured
that *Dear Eelephant, Sir* catalogues his penance
and recompense. Clive's debt is paid, now it is up
to us, our colleagues and countrymen in a new
South Africa to ensure that Clive's efforts were
not in vain and that his devotion to the wild will
continue to inspire us all.

ANTHONY HALL-MARTIN

22 JUNE 1992

Acknowledge-ments

My sincere thanks to Jane Zimmerman and Val Ford, who laboured over my early manuscripts and urged me to put it all down on paper and who assisted me in many of my wildlife ventures. To Libby Parker and Joe my thanks for valuable advice. To Sally Antrobus, who finally put it all together with such consummate skill and professionalism, I owe a special word of appreciation. To Louise Grantham, many thanks for support and encouragement.

To Anthony Hall-Martin, my thanks for writing the foreword. Anthony and I have shared many memorable moments among elephants.

To my family, who have endured my wanderings and adventures, my departures and homecomings, my joys and sorrows, my successes and failures (the pages of this book reveal only a glimpse), my mother Enid, my wife Conita, Renning, Anton and Constance, I express my deepest gratitude.

CLIVE H WALKER

MAY 1992

Dear Elephant, Sir

I write to you with a feeling of deep guilt and shame. In my youth I sought to kill your kind in some misguided belief that this brought me recognition in my world of intellect. Did I really enjoy what I did on that hot morning in the Moçambique bush, firing first into the head of a large one of your kind and then turning trembling to kill a young cow, who stood in fear as the herd stampeded in all directions in a panic to get away from that awful sound and human smell?

You ask me how I felt when watching an unsuspecting group of sixteen cows and calves advance towards gunmen in Hwange, to die in a shower of bullets; how I felt when I found the wind-and sun-scarred body of a lone cow, wounded by poachers, on a rock-strewn slope in Damaraland, or the chainsawed skull lying bleached on the banks of the Hoanib river in Kaokoland?

I'm told that some of us are too emotional, while others believe that you will have to pay your way into the twenty-first century with the hard currency of your ivory.

Your world diminishes and your kind fall back on the last wild regions. Will we find a place for you where vultures wheel in cloudless skies or do we plan to enclose you behind wire and concrete, shut away from the haunts of your bygone trails?

Elephant, Sir, we outnumber you: we have changed the face of your home and ours and now we play games by putting each into ever smaller compartments of our changing worlds.

We have written volumes down the ages about your greatness, and yet we seek to render you a mountain of rotting flesh with blood-filled eyes in the name of science and progress.

One day we may very well snuff ourselves out with our unforgivable neglect, yet self destruction is not inevitable. Your species has suffered considerably at the hands of mine and we in turn are equally inhumane towards one another.

And so dear Elephant, Sir, I apologise for our indifference and my past pursuits and hope you will understand that I am as guilty as the rest of my kind, for it seems we are jostling ourselves to death in our search for... what?

Perhaps some still see hope in the neglected dimensions of life, and perhaps we may pause to include you.
I hope so.

Your devoted friend

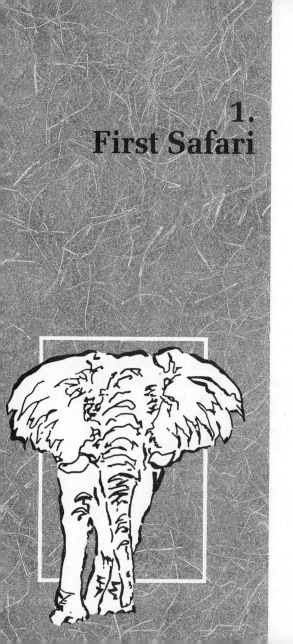

1.
First Safari

There is a lion skull sitting on my mantelpiece. It occupies a place of honor because it belonged to the man who launched my passion for the bush. He was born of German parents who lived in the Transvaal before the outbreak of the Anglo-Boer War. He became interested in the bush early on and began hunting in earnest. It was easy in those days; imprecise boundaries, no licences, almost no restrictions, and plentiful game. Even the Addo buffalo were there for the killing.

But Hans Bufe was not merely a killer of animals; he developed a great love for the veld and became an avid collector of Africana. He had the best collection of books on Africa's early days that I have ever come across. He also had a fine armoury, with a range of weapons that had me wide-eyed when I first saw it, and some double-barrelled express rifles that kicked the daylights out of you.

At our first meeting – I was about eighteen at the time – Hans told me bluntly that he would not take me out with him on a hunting safari until I had demonstrated my interest in the subject by first reading about it. He lent me two books, with instructions to read them within a week; then he would lend me two more.

This went on for some two years. I read two books a week and acquired more than a passing knowledge of the great hunters and pioneers of yesteryear. I was introduced to Selous, Baines and Livingstone, and was duly inspired. To me Hans himself was the embodiment of the heroic mould in which these men were cast, a cross between Selous and Ernest Hemingway. He was also a splendid storyteller who held me entranced with his hunting tales. It is my constant regret that I never recorded these narratives; they would have constituted an unparalleled record of southern African hunting history.

I can relate two elephant safari adventures I had with him myself, however. Two seemed to be the magic number for him. After two months of reading and tuition, Hans took me on my first hunting expedition. We travelled out to the Eastern Transvaal to what is today the Timbavati Game Reserve in his battered old Land Rover. There, with one of his rifles, I shot the very first animal in my hunting career, a blue wildebeest.

It would sound appropriate if I could say now that the experience revolted my sensibilities, but that would not be true. It did nothing of the sort. The truth is that I found it both exciting and exhilarating. The blood lust which stimulates hunters all over the world and which has been there since the dawn of time cannot be brushed

aside with a few pious words. The lust is powerful. Those who remember their first kill will readily understand the thrill I felt when that wildebeest dropped.

The poor animal got some posthumous revenge, however – ten days later I went down with the most severe case of tickbite fever imaginable. The experience taught me two invaluable things about the bush: first, that it can hand out some tough lessons and, second, that there is much more to hunting than merely peering down the scope of a rifle.

Hans Bufe got me back into his library and I continued to visit him once a week. Finally, when he felt I was ready for what he considered a real hunting safari, he arranged for me to go to Mozambique with three hunters. We travelled in a short-wheelbased Land Rover and a Willys Jeep into the dense bush somewhere north of the Olifants River and east of the Letaba region of the Kruger National Park. Herb Ririe, one of the men in our party, lent me a .93 Mannlicher, a medium calibre rifle not entirely suitable for big game, and it was with this weapon that I came to shoot my first elephant in 1957.

The thornveld of Mozambique east of the Kruger Park is thick, in some parts totally impenetrable. It was here that the two of us alighted from our vehicle and set off on the elephant trail, Herb armed with a .458 while I carried the much lighter Mannlicher. The herd we were tracking was moving slowly, so that by mid-morning we had caught up with them.

The bush was intensely hot and appeared to be covered by a green shimmering shield of solid heat. We crawled forward toward the noisily feeding herd until suddenly a very large bull loomed up in front of us. Although we were not really close enough to get in an effective shot, we were both sufficiently nervous – or at least I was – to fire. The bull went down with a tremendous crash and pandemonium broke out as the herd scattered, the elephants trumpeting and thundering in their effort to escape this deadly threat.

Our bull was nowhere to be seen. Instead, amid the deathly silence that replaced the noise of the departing herd, there stood a lone cow, frightened out of her wits.

We both fired, bringing her down instantly. This time I gazed down at the carcass of the animal and a sense of anti-climax enveloped me. True, the stalk had been exciting, but the end, it seemed to me, had been a big let-down. We never found the bull and we assumed he must have recovered and rejoined the retreating herd. Three

days later we shot a young bull and celebrated with beer bought at a Portuguese trading post. We drove back to the camp with a myriad of nightjars massed around the vehicle headlights. A beautiful mauve dominated the western sky ahead as I tried to digest the feeling of remorse that had begun to occupy my mind.

A year later, I hunted elephant with Hans Bufe and another companion, Bert Rademan, a senior airline pilot. It was May but still very hot. We had walked many miles and spent days tracking the giants about twenty kilometres from the Kruger National Park. Hans decided to go further north after some fresh elephant spoor, while Bert and I made for a thicket where we had been told by some villagers a herd was feeding. Rademan, a mild, amiable man, did not really want to shoot

at the water.

anything and was only there for the camp life and relaxation although he was an excellent hunter. But we found ourselves in dense bush where we had little hope of getting a shot in. With the herd somewhere ahead of us, loud but as yet invisible, the situation became rather frightening and Bert whispered in my ear: "Let's get the hell out of here!" I was delighted to agree and we crawled out and headed back to camp. On the way back, our Shangaan trackers pointed out some platforms overlooking the pans – erected by the Portuguese so that they could shoot elephants coming down to drink. I added this to my lexicon of perspectives on the sporting life.

A few days after this Hans returned and he and I set out along a trail which took us through a village. We questioned the villagers about elephant movements and were warned to be very careful. The elephants, they said, did not like people and were dangerous, but they gave us the information we needed and we set off on foot.

I love walking and have learned through experience that the best type of footwear for tramping in the bush is running shoes, not the good leather boots which I was then wearing. I found myself in difficulties, blisters welling up on my feet and each step more painful than the previous one. But I was naive enough to hide this from Hans for fear of losing face with the older man. Soon after-

wards, I forgot about my feet. Ahead of us were the elephant and we dropped to our hands and knees and crawled towards them, no easy task when you are toting a heavy Belgian rifle. Suddenly the wind changed and with a shrill scream a heavy grey object hurled itself at us. It was a terrifying moment. Gripped by fear, I made off in a crouch, desperate to escape the wrathful giant. But Hans was made of stronger stuff. He raised his rifle and as he did so the charging beast stopped short, turned, and crashed past me.

It was a cow and she was so close that I could clearly see her nervous brown eyes searching ahead. Hans lowered his rifle. He told me later that he never shot a cow unless his life was threatened. She veered off and rejoined the herd as our blood pressure slowly returned to normal. She had been just ten paces from us and we were very glad to see the last of her. Neither of us then understood the matriarchal structure of elephant society. All we were certain of was that a threatened cow can be the most dangerous animal and should be avoided at all costs. Years later I was to give evidence at an inquest into the death of a young woman who had been killed while trying to escape an enraged elephant cow.

Back in camp, after Hans left in search of more elephant, I was left alone and developed a serious case of blood poisoning, thanks to my raw and

bleeding feet. I lay on my stretcher and became delirious, feeling more wretched than I had ever felt in my life. Fortunately, Bert Rademan arrived and set about administering a penicillin injection. He had never done this before and after a few false starts, managed to sink the needle in and I felt somewhat better. I was unable to walk and the next morning Bert loaded me into the Land Rover and drove for fourteen hours nonstop to get me into a hospital. I decided there and then that I was a lousy elephant hunter.

Years later I was sent a tape recording by a total stranger whose father had known Hans Bufe: here follows the only other recorded adventure I know of involving this remarkable man.

The year was 1956. Bufe and a doctor companion, Bruce MacRae, were hunting on the Luangwa River in what was then Northern Rhodesia, and had had a hard day tracking buffalo. According to Bufe, MacRae had previously had a nasty experience on the horns of a wounded buffalo, and he now delighted in hunting them. MacRae had shot his buffalo and they had returned to camp at about four o'clock. Bufe announced that he was going to make a nice cup of tea, attend to supper, and then go out and shoot a crocodile.

Bufe set off to shoot his crocodile, which was in the habit of lying up on an island below the camp. He called the local wildlife department scout, named Chequenda, to assist him. Chequenda enquired after a boat but, much to his alarm, was informed that they would walk across the waist-deep river. Chequenda following reluctantly, Bufe duly shot the crocodile, which turned out to be a very large specimen. Chequenda summoned a squad of helpers who also enquired after a boat, but were told that as Bufe had killed the crocodile, they need have no fear. Halfway to the island, Bufe shouted, "Croc!" which elicited electrifying action, putting an ashen-faced group onto the island in seconds. They doubtless did not care too much for Bufe's sense of humour.

MacRae was not amused either, and reprimanded Hans for his stupidity in crossing a bilharzia- and crocodile-infested river, but Bufe never worried about such matters. During dinner they could hear lion down where they had skinned and opened up the crocodile. MacRae was reportedly stunned to think that such a noble beast would stoop to eat so lowly a creature as a crocodile. After MacRae had retired and Bufe sat cleaning rifles, there came the death bellow of a buffalo and the snarling of numerous lions. Bufe woke MacRae, suggesting that they go after the lion, which did not impress MacRae at all; by this

stage he was somewhat dubious about Bufe's suggestions. Chequenda was not too happy about wandering around in the dark with a torch, pointing out that it was against the law of the country anyway. But Bufe strode forth in search of the lions nonetheless.

After wandering unsuccessfully for a while by somewhat feeble torchlight, they listened out for the rapids in the river to find their way back. They could still hear the lions and decided to rise early the next day and try for them.

Before setting off at dawn, MacRae suggested a plate of porridge. Bufe refused, saying they could have that upon their return. Not seventy yards from camp they walked right into the pride of lions still feeding on a buffalo bull. Lions scattered to right and left. Bufe went after a big male which ran across an open vlei. He missed his first shot, but connected with the second as the lion entered the fringe of bush.

Proceeding very cautiously, they heard a roar from the lion whereupon Chequenda fired two shots, yelled, "The lion is coming!" – and turned and ran. The lion saw MacRae in the open and went for him in two great bounds. Bufe could not fire for fear of hitting the doctor, and the charging lion knocked MacRae to the ground and commenced mauling him. MacRae was a good rifle shot but missed twice as the lion charged down on him. Bufe said he realised afterwards that he had made a cardinal error by not leaving the wounded lion alone for half an hour or more so that the wound could slow down the animal. While the lion and MacRae were thrashing around Bufe thought, "My God, I mustn't shoot MacRae." He shot the lion further back along the body. In his anxiety to reload he jammed the bolt and was about to try to ram his rifle barrel down the lion's throat instead when the lion looked up, dropped MacRae, and went for Chequenda in two mighty leaps. As the animal brought the scout down, Bufe said all he could hear was Chequenda screaming, "Mama, mama help!" Clearing his head and the rifle action, Bufe shot the lion, which collapsed over the writhing Chequenda. Now Bufe saw MacRae trying to get up, a pitiable sight: one arm was badly broken and he was bleeding profusely from his side. Chequenda was in an even worse state, one arm hanging on by threads of skin – it was almost completely severed.

To Bufe's "Can I help you, Bruce?" MacRae replied, "Help Chequenda. He is in a worse condition than I am." Making a tourniquet from his handkerchief, Bufe bound MacRae's arm and ran back to camp to get his Land Rover to fetch Chequenda. He loaded blankets, mattresses, pillows, cushions and bandages into the vehicle and was in the act of reversing when the doctor walked unaided into camp.

Returning to Chequenda, Bufe applied a wire tourniquet to the arm, and then picked up the injured MacRae who had bandaged himself as well as he could, and left for help. Help was over eighty kilometres away and the two injured men must have suffered considerably over the rough terrain. The game scout had his arm amputated and MacRae lost a finger and suffered severe lacerations besides the broken arm.

When asked en route if there was anything he would like, MacRae told Bufe, "Yes. The plate of porridge I asked for this morning."

Before his death in 1974, Bufe gave me the skull of that lion, and I treasure it. Bufe was a true gentleman, quite prepared to sacrifice his own life in a tight spot for someone else's. In his day, he knew what wild country was all about. He knew the bush. Yet he did not know it in the way we do today. Love of the chase was strong in his veins. Today our sense of kinship with the wilderness rests on broader foundations. The lion skull on my mantel speaks volumes, but not the whole story.

2.
Ranger Days

I wondered why a stone moat surrounded the cemetery until my friend John Ilsley explained the reason. Elephant were frequent visitors here, and were in the habit of using the tombstones as rubbing posts. The only solution was to construct a barrier sufficient to keep the pachyderms out so that the ghosts of Tuli could rest in peace.

In 1966 the Tuli Block formed part of the British Protectorate of Bechuanaland, now Botswana. Little did I know then what an impact this place was to have on me in due course. At the time I had just started work there and was interested in learning what I could about the history of the area. Given its vastness and sparse population, one of the best resources in this regard seemed to be police records.

On my frequent trips to the Tuli Police Post, I had to pass the small cemetery on the bank of the river nearby. One day I stopped and wandered among the rows of graves. Who were these people? What had brought them here to die in the lonely sweltering backwoods of Bechuanaland? Each inscription told its own sad tale: "Killed by a lion and died near Tuli" . . . "Killed in action against the Boers at Pont Drift" . . . "Died of fever."

In the year 1890 an expedition, under the guidance of the renowned elephant hunter Frederick Courteney Selous, arrived on the banks of a broad sandy river which today forms the boundary between Botswana and Zimbabwe – the Shashe River, named after a Kalanga chief. The origin of the name comes from shaya-ishe, which means "lacking a chief", because the Kalangas at that time regarded their chief as useless. Selous thought he had reached the Tuli River – Tuli in turn is derived from the Shona word ubuthuli, meaning "river of dust"; it rises in the Matopos Hills and is a tributary of the Shashe River. The Shashe and the fort later to be built beside it became the gateway to Mashonaland and the country ruled over by King Lobengula of the Matabele.

The men of the expedition were enlisted as members of the Pioneer Column. Perhaps they stood and gazed across the broad expanse of dazzling white sand, and considered what had brought them to this strange land. The river would have been dry at the time of year they reached it. They may have wondered what the Matabele felt about the impending invasion of white men from the south in that year of 1890, although more likely they were cursing the heat and remoteness of the place. A great deal of blood was to flow during the following five years but none was shed on this expedition, which crossed the Shashe River and commenced its march to Mashonaland on July 11, 1890.

The Pioneer Column had come into being as a result of Cecil John Rhodes receiving royal assent to a charter for the British South Africa Company on October 29, 1889. Concessions were also granted to him by King Lobengula of the Matabele. Rhodes was permitted to search for gold in Mashonaland but on no account was he to enter Matabeleland. In any case this would have been impolitic because the concession he had been granted was unpopular with Matabele warriors in general, and there would have been armed opposition at the slightest pretext. The expedition therefore had to keep well away from Matabele country and Selous, who had visited Mashonaland before, planned a route to run well to the east of Lobengula's domain – although the king did claim lordship over all the tribes in this area.

Selous had thoroughly examined the country to the east of the Motloutse River and in May 1890 explored the terrain between the lower courses of the Motloutse, Shashe and Tuli rivers. He finally selected a good route for a wagon road that would be fairly well supplied with water all year and would cross the Tuli at a point about eight miles below its confluence with the Shashe, or so thought Selous. In fact the river that runs past the

fort *is* the Shashe. The river here passes close to a flat-topped hill which Selous saw as a strategic vantage point. And indeed Fort Tuli was later built here. Abandoned since the turn of the century, the fort lies in the eastern-most corner of Botswana, in the triangle bordered by the Shashe and Limpopo rivers. The only tribute to the pioneers at what remains of the silent fort on the road to Mashonaland is shattered glass and scattered iron. Many a secret lies forgotten in the peace and quiet of the surrounding mopane country. The fort commanded an excellent view of the river and was reasonably impregnable on three sides, being built on a rocky outcrop. The Shashe at this point is a sandy stretch some six hundred metres wide with clean, clear water running close to the fort side of the bank. In the rainy season the water comes down in a wild rush, sometimes rising twenty feet, but the flow lasts only a few days or weeks.

My first visit to Fort Tuli, towards the end of the rains in 1966, gave me pause as regards human foibles. I was curious about the place, and since the police post was across the river, my intention was to pay a courtesy call to the police as well. I set forth, accompanied by two of my staff who knew the way; I was not yet very familiar with the territory. After travelling for about an hour and a half over the most appalling road we passed a giant baobab tree, with a fresh clear

spring running nearby where we stopped to collect some water. As we rested there I noticed that the trunk of the baobab was covered with carved names and initials. My trackers could not help me with an explanation and I had to wait some time to learn who had journeyed before me on the hot dusty track past the baobab.

It was the original Rhodesian Pioneer Column of 1890, of course, led by Selous himself. The expeditionaries had camped beneath the tree, watered their horses, and marked their passing on the trunk of the baobab. One very clear name was that of W.E. Fry, the intelligence officer attached to the column. Today the tree is a national monument, a stone parapet protecting it from inquisitive elephants.

W.E. Fry was not alone in this impulse. Wherever they went in the wilderness, early explorers notched their names on trees. When Van Riebeeck climbed the forests on Table Mountain in 1652, even he discovered that others had been there before him: "In the former forests we found on a few trees the dates 1604, 1620 and 1622, so that they had already been found at that time, but by whom we could not determine," he recorded in his journal.

David Livingstone cut "DL" into a tree on an island in the Zambezi, and Baines, who followed him to the Victoria Falls, found this reminder that Livingstone had got there first. Livingstone is believed to have carved his name on a fig tree at Manyana, and although a number of branches have fallen off, the tree still stands. It was protected in the 1930s. When Livingstone died at Chitambo's village in 1873 a mobola plum tree (*Parinari curatellifolia)* was inscribed.

Dr. Livingstone
May 4th 1873
Chuma, Souza, Mniasere

On another excursion I found a baobab bearing the names of Boers of the Zoutpansberg Commando. Baobabs were certainly popular; across the Shashe River I found yet another with several names, one marked out with the spent shells of a Lee Enfield rifle. Did these men have anything to do with the Zeederburg Express, which had passed that way in 1891 en route to Bulawayo?

Rhodes is reputed to have carved his name on a mashatu tree, (*Xanthocercis zambesiaca)* on the banks of the Limpopo opposite what is today Baines' Drift. Tracking a wounded elephant at the confluence of the Shashe and Limpopo rivers

I discovered another kind of inscription – a marble tablet nailed to a *munye* tree (bird plum, *Berchemia discolor)*. It began: "As I walk through the wilderness of this world" and was placed in memory of a man who had lost his life in a naval disaster in 1918.

What sort of self-expression is this need to make our mark on trees? In the depths of Tuli, I had to assume it was a kind of territorial imperative: those travellers were the first whites to venture into country unexplored by their kind, and did not know what lay ahead, or if they would pass that way again.

A little unsure of my whereabouts, I did not linger long at the baobab near the spring, but continued down to the old Pioneer Drift on the Shashe River. Here the sight that met my eyes almost made me want to give up visiting the police. Compared to the Limpopo between Botswana and the Transvaal, this river was immense. The drift looked pretty firm, with clear flowing water which I judged to be about three metres wide and quite shallow. Stretching away to the opposite bank was clean, beautiful sand gleaming in the afternoon sun. I was greatly impressed by the amount of water in what I had expected to be a dry river.

Engaging low gear, I proceeded down the drift, intending to accelerate through the water to the firm ground. This turned out to be my undoing, however, as the Land Rover immediately sank into the sand. All efforts in various gear positions succeeded only in getting us bogged further and further down. When the water reached door level I conceded that the river had won the day. By this stage the three of us were drenched from kneeling in the water to examine the circumstances under our hapless vehicle.

Fortunately – by now the sun was fast sinking and the situation was somewhat embarrassing – on the opposite bank were some fifteen or so prisoners digging sand out of the riverbed under the watchful eye of a sergeant. I trudged across and prevailed upon him to come to our assistance.

Luck had it that the police were undertaking various building alterations, including a more sophisticated addition to their private bar – hence the river sand being required and our finding help so near at hand. My introduction to the river was embarrassing enough; I was relieved not to have had to walk up to the police post, introduce myself, and then ask an officer for help.

The Pioneers and those who followed in their wake must have had great difficulty in crossing the Shashe and Limpopo rivers in the rainy season, let alone the rivers they encountered in Mashonaland after leaving Fort Tuli. Moreover, with the rains came fever. During the wet season of 1890-91 there crawled a thin stream of prospectors, speculators, traders and the like, struggling with bullock transport to reach the promised land of gold. They did get there, most of them, after a weary journey of a thousand miles through Bechuanaland and southern Matabeleland. On the banks of the swollen rivers, little piles of stones were left to mark the last resting places of those whom fever and privation claimed as victims.

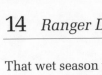

That wet season was very wet indeed and result-ed in a great hold-up of traffic at Tuli. Rivers were flooded and roads impassable so that at the fort there was an accumulation of stores, wagons, oxen, and impatient men. A community below the fort took on the semblance of a town. Today the only walls still standing are the remains of the jail. Hundreds and hundreds of smashed and broken bottles lie scattered about – not all whisky bottles, I imagine, but no doubt a good percentage of them are.

Adrian Darter recorded the following in 1896: "In later years the place acquired an evil name. It was the grave of good reputations, people said. Practically every man who remained there for a while lost the major part of any virtues he may once have possessed. But then much the same can be said of all those lonely little outposts where there was no society save the score of fever-stricken men who gathered nightly in some sweltering, tin-roofed canteen, no recreation save the drinking of so-called whisky, and no topic of conservation save the good luck of those who got away or the misfortune of those who died."

A peculiar feature of the area is that the boundary between Zimbabwe and Botswana, (from the point where the two meet South Africa at the Shashe confluence with the Limpopo), follows the course of the Shashe River north-westward

for several miles upstream toward the police post at Fort Tuli, but then describes an arc with a radius of ten miles into Botswana. Where the arc intersects the Shashe again, twenty miles further north-west, the Shashe again forms the interna-tional boundary. This came about in 1891 when the great Bechuana chief Khama granted a con-cession whereby native cattle had to be kept clear of the area within a radius of ten miles from the fort in order to protect trek oxen from the lung sickness that was rife among the Bamangwato herds at the time. That part of the circle beyond the west bank of the Shashe River became Zimbabwean territory and to this day is known as the Tuli Circle. The area is some 40 000 hectares in extent.

I was stationed across the border from Fort Tuli in Bechuanaland before independence was grant-ed in September 1966, as a ranger at a private game sanctuary of some ten thousand hectares. Besides fence-mending, shooting for the pot, and squiring my employer's family around on bush forays, my work included anti-poaching patrols.

In the course of my duties I came to keep an unof-ficial eye on the western portion of the Circle, as the ranger in charge was stationed some two hun-dred kilometres away at Beit Bridge and his game scouts were unable to patrol the area effectively. Poaching was always a problem in the Circle and poachers were in the habit of crossing our reserve to get there. Adrian Boshier, ranger at the Charter reserve at the opposite end of the Circle, looked after that side.

Life sometimes brings one into contact with wonderfully strange people. When I drove my Land Rover across the dry Shashe River into Rhodesia one day, heading again for the Tuli Police Post, I was about to meet one. Adrian was something of a legend by 1966. I had in fact taken over his post as ranger when he moved down to the south-eastern side of the Tuli Block near the border of South Africa. He became ranger for a small group of South Africans who owned land there, and had a reputation among locals of being thoroughly fearless.

Having struck up a friendship with the station commander at the Tuli post, I occasionally drove across on Saturday afternoons to swap information on poaching and to enjoy a beer bought in Gwanda through the police mess. Beer was expensive by comparison on our side since it had to come from Alldays, a dusty little Transvaal town fifty kilometres away. I earned the princely sum of one hundred rand a month, and after paying off fifty on my Volkswagen beetle, little enough was left for such luxuries as beer – although I would have forsaken various other items for the odd cold beer on a very hot after-noon down on the wide expanse of the Shashe River.

My introduction to Adrian took place at the police officers' quaint little bar atop the hill of Tuli. It was late afternoon when he strolled up, craggy, with a hawkish nose burnt brown by the Bechuanaland sun. His gaze was as strong as his handshake and I could not help thinking what a novice I was in comparison to this man. Adrian was tall, rugged with short-cropped hair, and very self-assured. I liked him, although I felt uneasy in his presence; I could not explain why. There was a mystery about this man and his ventures. He walked alone down the length of the Shashe River, unarmed except for a knife, living off animals he caught, and drinking the clean, clear water from the river.

We had been chatting and relaxing for some while. Adrian and I were on the customers' side of the bar and an officer was on the other side serving us, when Adrian suddenly picked up a police revolver and fired a shot into an unlikely wall light made of a wildebeest skull with a little red bulb glowing brightly inside – a fixture to give the place character, the police apparently thought. Head and bulb crashed down the wall, plunging us into darkness. For good measure, Adrian also put a shot through the corrugated iron roof of the building. At this point we retired

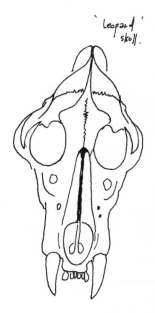
`Leopard`
skull.

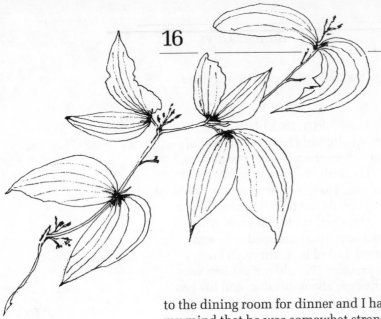

to the dining room for dinner and I had made up my mind that he was somewhat strange.

The talk turned to terrorism, as guerilla warfare used to be called. Adrian, anxious to demonstrate what he would do if a terrorist suddenly walked into the room, picked up his beer can and with great force hurled it down the passage, where it bounced noisily off the corrugated iron walls. At precisely this point the mess orderly came around the corner carrying our soup. The missile somehow missed him and ended up in the toilet. Sadly, our soup wound up on the floor. Adrian concluded his demonstration by leaping up and grabbing me in a vice-like headlock, from which it took two officers no little effort to extricate me.

I felt it prudent to retire to bed, somewhat shaken. Early in the morning I quietly slipped away, leaving Adrian sound asleep on the verandah, and disappeared back to Bechuanaland as quickly as I could drive my Land Rover, not even pausing to thank my hosts.

Boshier was an enigma. My first meeting with him was a revelation, to say the least. He certainly was both feared and admired by the local population; his loathing of poachers and the treatment he meted out to them was legend. He was an excellent ranger and master at bushcraft. He felt strongly about the Tuli and it must have been with a very heavy heart that he finally had to abandon the place he loved. Once Bechuanaland became Botswana, his methods of dealing with poachers became unacceptable to the authorities and he swiftly left, never to return again legally. He did return on occasion, however, slipping across the Limpopo from the Transvaal to walk through his beloved Shashe woodland, home of the Tuli elephants, and then quietly made his way back across the Limpopo into South Africa.

One of his methods of extracting information from poachers who were not forthcoming was to lock them up in a hut and threaten to slip in some deadly snake to hasten their answers. It worked. He caught many poachers in the thorn and ilala thickets of Tuli. His exploits would fill a book; mine are mild interludes in comparison.

Once I was with Harry Miller the manager of the reserve at which I worked, deep in the Tuli Circle, when out of the blue sky dropped a helicopter which landed in a clearing close by. Adrian emerged and the helicopter took off again. He had no idea that we were there, yet he showed no surprise when we called out his name. What he thought we were doing I'll never know, but he was seeking a likely place for a film sequence involving charging elephants in a movie about the Kruger millions. The exercise nearly cost a cameraman his life because he failed to heed Adrian's advice to stay with his camera and, if the going became really rough, to step behind an adjacent large tree. The cameraman lost his nerve at the sight of a charging elephant, and fled. Fortunately no harm befell him.

I was not to see Adrian again for many years. But the ghosts of this triangle of land bordered by great rivers, steeped in history of hunters, missionaries, adventurers and pioneers, must surely have embraced the spirit of Adrian Boshier after he lost his life in a diving incident on the Zululand coast in 1978. Lyall Watson's book *Lightning Bird* is an account of the life of this extraordinary Englishman who ventured into the remote regions of southern Africa, lived for many years in the bush and delved deeply into the mysteries of tribal witchcraft, prehistoric artifacts, and ancient rock art.

The reserve where Harry and I worked belonged to a Johannesburg family. A not uncommon pursuit of South Africans then, as now, was owning a piece of bushveld. More often than not owners knew very little about managing a game reserve, but loved to indulge in the luxury of having their own reserve. In those days I knew about as little as they did, but I have since come to realize how ignorant many were about sound veld management. Seeing lots of game was viewed as more important than worrying about the condition of the veld. The eastern Tuli Block was no exception in the 1960s. You either hunted or enjoyed watching your plentiful game. In our case the only hunting we did was for rations. Vast sums of money were spent on glamorous camps and amenities but there was little concern about local ecology.

Building camps did nothing for me. I sought every moment to get out into the bush. I also formed a lasting frienship with one of the four trackers working for me. Johannes Naari taught me a great deal about the bushveld. He was later to become an outstanding tracker and expert on elephant behaviour. Together Johannes and I and Bush Willem Naari, his uncle, patrolled the area,

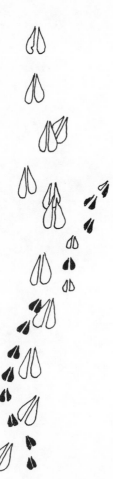

encountering poachers and elephants. We had some memorable experiences which had a lasting impact on my thinking, and did much to develop my feeling for wild country.

Poachers. We use the word to describe people who kill game illegally, often, in a cruel fashion, and occupy the attention of most game rangers at one time or another. In recent years these people have come to be armed with automatic weapons, chainsaws and the like, but it wasn't like that in the 1960s. Even most organized poachers then were only in small commercial rings, taking advantage of the fact that the authorities had few police to spare to enforce anti-poaching laws during the transition from the Bechuanaland Protectorate to the Republic of Botswana. Landowners had to do their own enforcement.

Poaching is nothing new. History records this ancient crime. What we often forget is that in most cases it is a matter of human survival. What must it be like to be a peasant living adjacent to a well-stocked national park or game reserve? It's easy to be smug and regard poachers as common criminals when you don't have to worry about where the next meal is coming from.

My first encounter with poachers was not very successful. I am sure that they knew we were after them, got the drop on us, and simply vanished. Like most poachers in our area, they came from Rhodesia with donkeys, which they walked in the tracks of zebra. It was an old trick, meant to throw us off the trail by eliminating their spoor. The donkeys were to transport the meat out. We eventually found their camp well into the Tuli Circle and surprised two men, one skinning an impala and one collecting water nearby.

Racing forward, we called on them to stand still, whereupon the man skinning the impala dashed over to a homemade gun and fired at almost point blank range at Bush Willem and me. A strange sensation: I had no idea what kind of ammunition was in that ancient weapon. I fired back over his head, and he made off at high speed toward the river with the two of us in hot pursuit. But he knew more about survival than we did, and he was soon lost in the deep riverine vegetation.

The second poacher stood dead still and was quickly handcuffed. We confiscated three bags of dried meat and a number of impala skins. With mild threats we made him show us where their snares were laid out. We recovered well over forty. We bundled poacher, snares and meat into my Land Rover and got back to camp well after dark. Boshier had handcuffed poachers to a large leadwood tree when he worked here and to a length of chain around this tree we duly secured our poacher for the night. I found his silence and gaze disturbing. He had given up with no fight; no doubt this was not his first experience. The following morning I intended to transfer him across the Circle to the Rhodesians at the Tuli Police Post.

By dawn he was gone. How, we had no idea, but after tracking him to the Rhodesian border and finding our handcuffs discarded on the side of the track, we decided that one of our people must have assisted in his getaway. Naturally no one had the faintest idea . . . Thereafter we made certain that poachers were taken to the police post and not to our camp. I of course felt a complete idiot at my first prisoner's escape, and wondered how Adrian would have handled the matter.

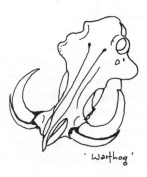

'Warthog'

Bordering the Tuli are the tribal lands of the Bamangwato where hunting was legal and was carried out on a large scale. Trapping was also legal on tribal lands, but inevitably spilled over into the wildlife-rich reserves. Lions are fairly common along the Shashe River, and were no exception when it came to being caught in steel traps known as slagysters. Traps were set out to catch not only lion, but leopard as well. Hyaena were regular victims too. When trapped, an animal often suffered for days before the trapper turned up to put it out of its misery. Lions usually got the blame from locals for cattle losses and traps were then set to put a stop to their depredations. All too often it was the skin which was in fact being sought, since lion and leopard skins fetched very high prices.

A recognised crossing between Rhodesia and the tribal lands was at the confluence of the Shashe and Tuli rivers, near the Mokosha cattle post in the tribal lands. Poachers stopped over here before setting off to lay snares in the Tuli Circle or private game reserves. With the help of John Ilsley, the police officer at Baines' Drift down on the Limpopo, we had earlier raided this cattle post and arrested a poacher complete with snares and impala skins.

A month later Johannes Naari and I were on a routine patrol. Near the boundary between the

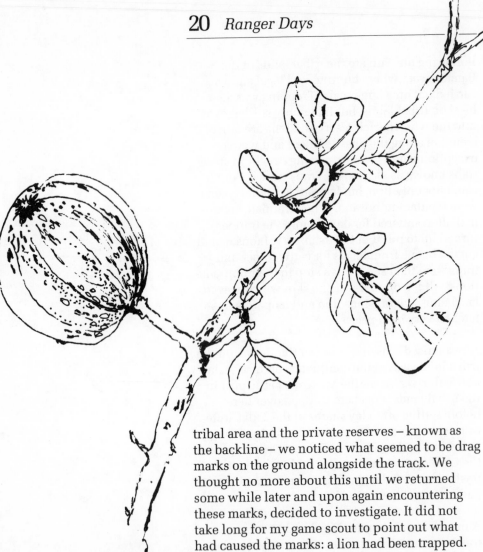

We found where he had been caught, below the remains of an impala ewe wedged into the fork of a mopane tree. In his efforts to reach the impala, the lion had stepped into the trap hidden at the base of the tree. Judging by his spoor, there appeared to be a log attached to the trap. He had had great difficulty in dragging this about and had gone around in circles tearing up grass and bushes. What puzzled us was our finding another spot where, judging from the devastation of the bush, another lion had been trapped. Later we were to learn that another lion had indeed been caught previously in the same trap and had eventually freed himself, but not without leaving one of his paws behind. He became a great menace.

That first lion terrorised the area considerably. One night he killed a dog in front of its master's hut, and then a young heifer. Only by the firing of an abandoned hut and much shouting and beating of tins was he finally driven off. Another night at an irrigation scheme camp, a Rhodesian police officer encountered the same lion. This time he did not cause any trouble, in spite of the fact that there were donkeys present. He drank from the swimming pool and left, much to the relief of the police officer. Presumably he had fed well on someone else's donkey. Morning revealed his pug marks, clearly showing only three impressions with just a faint smudge indicating where the missing paw should have been.

tribal area and the private reserves – known as the backline – we noticed what seemed to be drag marks on the ground alongside the track. We thought no more about this until we returned some while later and upon again encountering these marks, decided to investigate. It did not take long for my game scout to point out what had caused the marks: a lion had been trapped.

Thus handicapped, he made goats and donkeys his regular prey, but he did make a kill on one occasion inside an abandoned roadworks camp surrounded by thorn bushes which had long since fallen into decay. The prey was an impala ram which was found on examination to have been diseased. The kill was fresh and I lay up in hope of the lion's return, but to no avail. Eventually the livestock killing ceased and he troubled people no more. He had either gone across the river into Rhodesia, or possibly fallen, in desperation for food, into a baited trap once more.

The lion we were following now had made off into deep bush bordering the river, continually recrossing his own spoor. We were discussing his progress and possible whereabouts when he suddenly decided to show himself. He had been lying up in some dense bush and had heard us gradually getting nearer. He could no longer remain silent at our intrusion and with a deep growl came charging out of the thicket, dragging the trap. Even though his rush was considerably slowed by the trap and log, he was enormous as he rushed forward in a blind, awful rage. Sheer terror gripped me. I did manage to shoot, causing him to retreat into dense cover. My rifle was equipped with a knockdown telescopic sight which came off with the recoil, catching me a glancing blow in the face. He was obviously much hampered by the trap and weakened by his

struggle to free himself, and this probably saved us from serious injury.

We retreated to the Land Rover and waited for about twenty minutes, smoking Johannes's President cigarettes. My nerves were somewhat jangled at this stage and my hands trembled. I had had a stirring bout of real fear. We cautiously made our way back up the river to where we thought he lay, and tried to pick him out in the gloom. Soon we were rewarded with the clink of chain and a low growl. Climbing a tree, I was able to see him in a slight hollow, his back to me Silently motioning to Johannes for the rifle, I hastily put that lion out of further agony.

Upon examination, we found the trap securely clamped onto one paw. Later four of us were unable to release the trap using our combined strength, and eventually we had to open it with steel clamps. In his effort to free himself the lion had broken his jaw and a number of teeth, one canine in particular being very badly smashed. No bones were broken in the paw, the teeth of the trap having locked between the knuckles. Just how many days he had been trapped was anyone's guess. The trapper, after setting the trap, had returned to his village some thirty miles away. He and a helper were apprehended the following day by two government game scouts on suspicion of using snares (not, unfortunately, for

'knobthorn'

trapping lions). He still had the first lion's paw on him when he was arrested.

I later received a letter from one of the game scouts who had caught the lion trapper: "I brought two African males before the native authority on Wednesday 20th July 1966. They are fined as follows: Mogapi Patani – R4,00. The one who caught the lion by the trap." Small wonder that soon after paying his fine he probably set off straight away to trap some other lion. The fine could hardly have deterred him. That game scout was John Benn, whom we met as we were returning to camp with the dead lion. He was peddling a bicycle along the dusty Tuli track with his .458 strapped to its crossbar. He was later to become regional warden of Ngamiland.

Villagers at Mokosha showed the poacher, Patani, where I had shot his lion. After he had paid his fine, he laid a charge against me for assault and for taking his trap and lion skin! (The assault

charge arose from my allegedly throwing his bike on top of him as he left my vehicle after I had given him a ride one day.) He was demanding return of the skin and trap, but I was in no frame of mind to oblige and nearly found myself in jail as a result. John wrote me a number of letters which I studiously ignored, for I was still furious about what I considered cruel and totally unnecessary actions. I was naive, of course, and over-zealous, for this had been going on for years and years, and was legal in the tribal areas, and it was white traders who sold these traps in the first place.

Lest I give the impression that my ranger days were all high adventure and historical rambling, let me add that much of that time spent in the Tuli was peaceful and solitary. It was there that I began to experiment with Indian ink on white paper, spending the long evening hours alone in camp, painting. Some of the time was even romatic. By a kind of miracle, considering my isolation, it was while I worked as a ranger in the Tuli that I met my wife to be, Conita. She was bridesmaid at the wedding of my former flying instructor, Dickie Dobson, and I was best man. I'm not quite sure to this day why she opted for me, since my worldly possessions at the time consisted of an Alsatian, the Volkswagen beetle, a collection of Africana books, some art materials, and one hunting rifle.

And it was there that my absorption with elephants began to run deep. I learned, for example, that at night they seem to loose their fear of people. Once, as we were escorting a captured poacher back to our vehicle some kilometres away, Johannes and I walked into a small herd of elephant in fading light and stepped up our pace nervously, but unnecessarily.

Later, near the home which Adrian Boshier had built of wood and stone, I walked among elephant on a moonlit night with Johannes and his young wife. It was a strange, silent, ghostly experience. We got right into a fair-sized herd feeding on ilala palms which grew in abundance there. Grey shapes like silent yachts passed us as we flitted from cover to cover. No sound was made by the elephant other than the sharp snapping off of the palms as they fed. The only noticeable sign that they had detected our presence was their slightly quickened pace as each one passed us. Years later I found the same when on foot at night with Lloyd Wilmot in the Okavango, walking among elephant. It is quite extraordinary how they ignore you. Perhaps they understand that man, the great destroyer, is nearly undone by the terrors of darkness. We were as safe as the occupants of the stone-moated cemetery.

Waterbuck 07

3.
Getting into Wildlife

Dennis Groves had a great passion for reptiles, the living kind, although he also had numerous snakes and chameleons in jars of methylated spirits. It was the bottled ones that attracted me. I was not that comfortable with the living variety and to this day I am not; I have had my fair share of frights.

My first recollection of an interest in wildlife is linked to my friendship with Dennis at Jeppe Preparatory School, and to youthful visits to the Johannesburg Zoo. After my father died in 1944 I moved to Treverton Boarding School near Mooi River, and here I had my first opportunity to get out into the country in earnest. During the polio epidemic in 1948 my brother and I spent three months on a dairy farm in the Mooi River district. I learned how to shoot guinea fowl, although most of the time I suffered more than the guinea fowl did. I also learned to ride a horse, broke some bones, and befriended Gary Player's step brother, Chris Goldsworthy, who talked glowingly about Ian having become a game ranger. A boy's dream. How was I to achieve that? Treverton – long after I had left – became the first school in South Africa to include environmental studies in the school curriculum, mainly through the efforts of Don Richards. Treverton was also to hold the first conference on environmental studies and has become internationally recognised for its work.

After high school I took to studying art, which I had begun to do at Treverton. The chances of becoming a game ranger seemed remote; I had neither connections nor experience. But one connection was soon to develop. Meeting Hans Bufe – elephant hunter, storyteller, traveller – at last got me out into the bush proper. Hans, however, between hunting and Africana tutorials, was always telling me to forget about becoming a game ranger. "Develop your art," he would say, "and forget about dreaming". I never could give up dreaming, but 1959 found me sailing for England – hardly the place for game ranger training – with the idea of staying a year. After travelling around Europe for six weeks, I arrived back in London with just enough cash for a month's rent in a room for two above the old Overseas Visitor's Club. My roommate was a wild Australian who played professional rugby and was rarely home. He left after two months and his place was taken by a New Zealander who was to become a life-long friend: Alan Stevens, a short, wiry man, very good at cross-country running.

Twice I fell for invitations to join him at it. The first time I had to remove tennis shoes which were killing me, halfway through the cross-country course, and we sped off up a wooded lane lined with chestnut trees, with an ample supply of *prickly* chestnuts on the muddy pathway. The second time was at Hyde Park one fog-shrouded day. Alan was a good hundred metres ahead of me in the sound-deadening fog when two cavalry officers tore past on either side of me, mounted on enormous horses. My heart did resume beating, but that was the end of my running career. The only running I have done since has been to get away from rhinos and elephants.

On that London sojourn I took Hans's advice of pursuing art. Often I visited the British Museum of Natural History and felt thoroughly homesick every time I peered up at the mounted elephants. After a spell as a dish washer (short-lived as two of us were nabbed at midnight making milk shakes so mountainous that the mix became detached from the machine and most wound up on the ceiling) I was offered a post as a wine steward by the late Max Wilson of the O.V.C. In due course I found myself second in charge of the club's bars, which was fun, paid the rent, and gave me a chance to meet many interesting people and to continue my art.

We had some wildlife in the club in the shape of a South American macaw called Max and took no little delight in occasionally taking him out of his cage in the Grotto Bar and launching him down the length of the place, claiming that he had escaped accidentally. A macaw trying to land in a narrow restaurant was an experience most diners didn't care for. He would attempt a forced landing on a crowded dinner table with the most spectacular results, whereupon we would arrive on the double, apologising profusely, and return the screeching parrot to his cage.

Travel was what the O.V.C. was all about and Max Wilson did things in a big way. In the early 1960s he chartered entire liners from the Union Castle Steamship Company and many of us had the good fortune to act as hosts on board, which provided us with an economical way of travelling, as well as a sound background in tourism. In 1961 I returned to South Africa on one such voyage down the east coast of Africa, a magnificent six weeks, which included a week in Mombasa. There I had my first venture as a safari guide.

Five of us – three girls, a Rhodesian tobacco farmer, and I – hired an Opel station wagon and set off loaded with provisions for Tsavo National Park. I don't recall the number of black rhino we encountered there but they were common enough. Once we were nearly hit by an irate rhino we had scared half to death. Black rhino have all but disappeared from Kenya today.

Zebra at speed.

White faced owl!

I returned permanently to South Africa in 1963 and went into the advertising world, although by now I wanted a life among the animals of Africa more than anything else. With the aid of a civil aviation grant, I took my private pilot's license. My flying instructor, the late Frank Lister, taught me how to fly a two-seater Piper Cub. From this I graduated to a 150 Cessna and to a Tiger Moth, and finally received wings under the tutorship of Dickie Dobson, later to become a senior pilot with Trek Airways. After two years of working, flying and collecting books, life took a dramatic turn. Through a mutual acquaintance, I was introduced to John McKenzie Johnson, who owned a game lodge in the Tuli Block. He needed an assistant game ranger and, after a brief interview, he offered me the job.

Dennis Groves' purpose in life manifested itself early. From his boyhood of bottled reptiles, he was to become the first curator of the Transvaal Snake Park. Ours was an era when a passionate interest could still become a way of life. Today you pretty well have to take a wildlife management degree or nature conservation diploma to make any headway in the field, and no doubt that's for the best, greatly improving the formal background of those entering upon careers devoted to wildlife. My own progress toward such a career was sporadic and idiosyncratic, not precisely the sort of route I'd recommend. But the field was open, the needs many, and opportunities not too hard to find.

Thus began my life as a full-time wildlife man. Working as game ranger in the Tuli Block meant I encountered elephant in large numbers in an environment which allowed me to study them at close range. They were a jittery bunch, as elephants go, because they had gathered in the Tuli under human pressure from three countries. But it was here, dear Elephant, Sir, that I learned to know your kind.

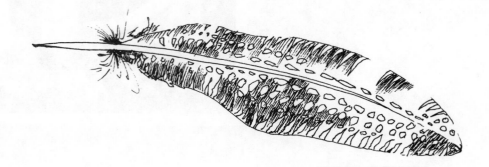

4.
The Prodigious Provider

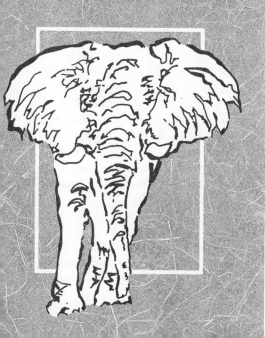

The fax from the World Wide Fund for Nature in Lausanne, Switzerland said: "Today the parties to the International Convention in International Trade in Endangered Species of Wild Fauna and Flora (CITES) voted overwhelmingly to place the African elephant on Appendix I." This meant that the elephant was officially regarded by CITES as an endangered species, as of October 1989. For signatories to the convention this banned outright all trade in any of the animal's products – ivory, meat, hair or hide.

An endangered species! What are we doing? How did it come to this? Why, I am frequently asked, is there so much concern about the African elephant? Why is the African elephant regarded as this continent's most valuable animal against the claims of so many other species? Why classify it as endangered when there remain upwards of half a million?

In simple economic terms, the elephant is immensely profitable. A few African countries have already come to grips with this. An elephant is a prodigious provider – of meat in huge quantity; ivory bringing great price; even the skin is of enormous value. And, of course, as a tourist attraction the elephant is invaluable. In 1990 alone, Botswana earned some $92 million from its tourist trade and the elephant, as an attraction, accounted for a good part of that amount.

For many, there is more to it than that, however. The elephant is a gift from nature. We have plundered them and shot them without the least regard for the consequences. A century ago, there were at least three million elephants in Africa. Little more than a decade ago, there were still more than a million. Today, we are down to perhaps three quarters of a million, and the numbers are still steadily dropping. The majority of elephants will eventually be concentrated in southern Africa, because in many countries to the north they have been so wantonly destroyed.

The first problem lies in the fact that the majority of elephants on this continent live outside protected areas. This unfortunate situation locks them into a constant struggle for survival against the forces of poverty, greed and corruption in the rapidly expanding human populations surrounding them. The odds stacked against these elephants seem insuperable. In a decade from now, the human population will have doubled and, with better education and upliftment, its demands upon natural resources will have trebled or worse. Even in game reserves and national parks, governments have studiously ignored the real cost of protecting valuable animals. More importantly, they have never come to terms with the needs and aspirations of deprived communities living in and adjacent to these sanctuaries.

It is a fact of recent history that indigenous people in Africa have been excluded from most of the benefits derived from conservation areas, and only governments, tourists or licensed professional hunters have stood to gain. The potential for rural communities to assist authorities in protecting rhino and elephant has been disastrously neglected. Where rural communities have been given the chance to share some of the benefits of proper wildlife management, as in Namibia's Kaokoveld, KwaZulu, Zimbabwe and, most recently, Zambia, their co-operation has proved immeasurably valuable.

For most of my adult life I have been deeply involved with elephants. Here is a creature which, in so many ways, is very much like us, with sophisticated social organization and complex patterns of communication. The elephant is highly intelligent and extremely adaptable; it uses plenty of resources for its daily sustenance – and yet, in a region like the Kaokoveld, can survive with the barest minimum, trekking sixty kilometres a day in search of water. As long as people refrain from shooting them, elephants will continue adapting and surviving.

I am sitting on the bank of the dry Sand River in the Sabi-Sand game reserve. A grey-headed bush shrike and a piet-my-vrou call persistently and I hear the lone cry of a fish eagle. The vegetation is green beneath a lowering grey sky. A puffback shrike calls "twerrup twerrup!" to my right and a little way in front of me lies the fresh dung of an elephant. A broken marula tree hangs limply on my left and up and down the river is more evidence of elephant.

In 1974, there were only six elephants in this 56 000-hectare reserve, adjoining the western boundary of the Kruger National Park. As I write, there are forty-three, introduced from the Kruger Park. When the idea of bringing in young elephants which had been spared from culling in the Kruger was first suggested, there was strong opposition. But John and Dave Varty, owners of the Londolozi game reserve which lies within the Sabi-Sand, went ahead anyway. Thirty-two young animals were brought in, of which five were killed by lions and three made their way back to the Kruger. Once in company with Dr. Anthony Hall-Martin, senior research officer in the Kruger Park, I encountered two of these. Both youngsters wore collars emitting radio signals on the Londolozi frequency.

The Vartys were among the very few owners of private property in the Eastern Transvaal who were keen to accept young elephants orphaned by family group culling in the Kruger Park. Most landowners are reluctant to face the damage the giants can cause. They are also, understandably

perhaps, scared of the beasts. A charging elephant is a pretty intimidating sight.

And yet it is wrong to assume that a charging elephant is bent on death and destruction. Most charges are simply warnings to encroachers to keep their distance. Too often the term "rogue" is applied and property owners call urgently on the wildlife authorities to have the animal put down. On the other hand, an elephant can be extremely dangerous when it feels itself threatened. A cow with young, for instance, will not hesitate to confront anyone who gets too close. Even then, however, the intruder usually receives ample warning to keep well away from a breeding herd before the elephant defence is pressed to a decisive conclusion. The trouble is that we are often more frightened of elephants than they are of us, so we shoot first, and the term "rogue" then comes too easily to our lips as justification.

Secretary bird

Indeed, it is precisely their size, strength and intelligence which, paradoxically, have made elephants so vulnerable. The prodigious provider can also be an impressive destroyer. At times they present a threat to human existence. Africa's villagers are no strangers to the problem of having to flee their homes in the face of advancing elephants trampling their property and eating their crops.

To be sure, elephants can be a nuisance even if you aren't a subsistence farmer. I recall a night when a bull elephant walked through a camp fence and ate the tempting Indian bamboo (which should not have been growing there in the first place) and some aloes. The bamboo had been planted there by an owner who yearned for the wilderness but brought garden trappings to it. When the bull had finished with the decorative vegetation, he turned his attention to the tap in the garden. Scenting the lovely water, he proceeded to destroy the fixture and wallow in the glorious mud which 5 000 litres of tapwater created.

Another incident I saw was to the north of the Klaserie game reserve, where a landowner was being harassed by a persistent gatecrasher. This elephant would pay a nightly call and had pulled on the garden hose with such force that the tap and pipes were yanked out of shape. He made himself a nuisance in other ways and it was finally decided that a stone wall a metre high and half again as thick might discourage the huge grey jumbo from pestering the household. These people were in for a surprise. The elephant climbed that wall without much trouble and had to be peppered with birdshot in the rear before he finally took the hint to depart.

All incidents do not end in mud wallows or birdshot, however. A few years ago, wildlife law enforcement officers were sent to investigate when an elephant broke through the south boundary fence into the Klaserie from an adjoining farm, whence the complaint came. Unable to raise the Klaserie warden on the radio, the officers entered the reserve and duly shot the problem animal. The row that developed caused an unprecedented uproar which reverberated for several years.

The warden, Erwin Leibnitz, telephoned me and I promptly arranged with Will Bernard of the SABC's "Radio Today" programme for a broadcast which included interviews with the warden, the authorities and myself. The ensuing publicity aroused the public considerably, and the Transvaal Directorate of Nature Conservation had a difficult time explaining the action taken by its officers. To the warden and me it seemed highhanded; the death of that elephant could have

been prevented. Many people living in the area were incensed, believing that too many elephants were being shot. In this instance the head office authorities knew nothing about the shooting, which left us feeling that the men in the field did as they pleased.

All things considered, though, this was a first-rate storm in a teacup – except for the elephant. Shooting one bull made no difference to the overall elephant population. Probably five hundred elephants were culled in the neighbouring Kruger Park that year. But the force of public reaction across South Africa illustrated a home truth about elephants: the powerful emotional response people have toward them.

That response is why elephants are at the top of the tourist shopping list in African game parks. The value in tourist-dollar terms of a living elephant is incalculable. At last this is being acknowledged, when the sands are running through the hour glass and it is already five minutes to midnight. Imagine Kenya without any elephants. She would lose many tourists and considerable income. Little wonder then, that Kenya made the dramatic and very wasteful demonstration of burning all stored ivory.

The West has become almost hysterical in its sudden concern for the elephant, applying as usual western ideology upon Third World realities. To list the elephant as endangered and ban the ivory trade is not going to solve the problem. It may slow the rate of elephant decline, but it will not put an end to a trade that has flourished for more than two thousand years.

On the face of it, Africa has enlisted the support of the West to fight the ivory battle, but emotion blinds people to the real issue: to protect these animals properly is going to cost a great deal of money. The available habitat for elephants in national parks and protected areas can accommodate only about a third of the 625 000 elephants still expected to be surviving in a few years' time. Over a total range of half a million square kilometres, African elephant protection will cost, at present values, something in the region of $100 million a year if the job is to be done properly. Where will this money be found?

The irony is that the sale of culled ivory from the well managed southern African elephant populations substantially funds the parks in which those animals thrive and multiply until judicious culling becomes imperative. Loss of revenue from necessary elephant culling and sale of products in southern Africa will seriously jeopardise present levels of protection unless alternative sources of funding are found. Involvement of rural communities would certainly help. So would the revenue derived from increased park fees as charged today in Botswana, provided they are ploughed back into the conservation system or go to benefit the rural communities adjacent to sanctuaries. Perhaps the tourists to African game parks would be happy to pay a surcharge to protect the world's heritage of elephants? Perhaps the West might undertake to share the financial burden for a change?

As I write this, someone, somewhere, is illegally killing an elephant. It is anyone's guess where the elephant population will level off; I'm afraid the popularly estimated 625 000 is too much to hope for. Countries which are fast losing their elephants will somehow have to be persuaded to accept responsibility themselves, rather than blaming ivory dealers and Oriental craftsmen who don't know the blunt from the sharp end of an elephant, and don't care anyway.

THE CHARGE.

M&N HANHART CHROMO LIT

Elephants have been under siege in southern Africa for almost 300 years (Photograph courtesy Africana Library)

Frederick Courteney Selous epitomised the early naturalist hunters. (Photograph courtesy The Star)

COPYRIGHT BARNETT

▼ *Clive Walker and trackers with his first elephant kill in Mozambique in 1957*

▲ *Hunter Hans Bufe introduced the author to the ways of the wild*

John Benn, a tracker in
the Tuli Block, later became warden
of Ngamiland in Botswana

Johannes Naari was teacher, guide
and mentor to Clive Walker

Mokabela, a Bayei elder and master Okavango guide

Clive Walker and Johannes Petou with the skull of a buffalo snared in the Tuli enclave

Lloyd Wilmot is notorious for his close encounters with elephants

▼ *David Shepherd with the remains of an elephant fatally wounded by poachers (Photograph courtesy David Shepherd)*

▲ *The rotting carcass of a hunter's prey*

The fury of an elephant cow in full charge

The author with Professor Koos Bothma, the first recipient of EWT support

▲ Clive Walker with Dr Iain Douglas-Hamilton, champion of elephant conservation in Africa

A Kaokoland desert elephant in the Hoanib River

▲ Clive and Conita Walker (Photograph courtesy Frank Black)

▼ Lloyd and June Wilmot's unconventional wedding on the banks of the Savuti Channel

Councillor Alan Gad congratulates the author on the opening of Clive Walker House (Photograph courtesy Frank Black)

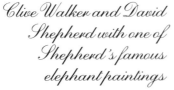

Clive Walker and David Shepherd with one of Shepherd's famous elephant paintings

▲ *President Lucas Mangope receives the first EWT Stateman's Award from chairman Ken Whyte (Photograph courtesy Frank Black)*

▼ *Lucky Mavrandonis has always been a champion fundraiser for conservation*

Standard Bank
ISANDO

The Standard Bank of South Africa Limited
Die Standard Bank van Suid-Afrika Beperk

01-25-42-43

Pay
Betaal   Endangered Wildlife Trust   17/11/85

R 8300-00

LAGAMED (PTY) LTD

▶ Peter Joffe surveys the
mummified remains of
an elephant killed by
poachers in the
Kaokoveld

▶▶ Conservation relies
heavily on
fundraising drives

▲ Dr Mangosuthu G. Buthelezi, President of the Rhino and Elephant Foundation, talking to Clive Walker (Photograph courtesy George Allen)

▼ The founders of the Rhino and Elephant Foundation (from left to right) Peter Hitchins, Dr Anthony Hall-Martin and Clive Walker

An elephant track at a dried waterhole

Elephant research – Kaokoveld
University of Pretoria and
Endangered Wildlife Trust.

5.
Full Circle

To me, a love for people is an essential qualification for a wildlife conservationist. People who shut themselves off from most of humanity – or who develop misanthropic tendencies, as many who want to live and work in the bush are inclined to do – cannot be an effective force in conserving our natural heritage. Conservation, by its very nature, is a people business, not an ideal to be pursued in isolation. It is *for humanity* that we must conserve and protect our environment; it is people who must learn to love their world. Ultimately it is a matter of human survival, nothing less.

More than thirty years ago, I learned the sorry truth that while the hunters of yesteryear may have been cast in a heroic mould, hunting could bring out the worst in people too. And I saw that this form of interaction with the wilds had severe limitations.

On one Mozambique safari in the 1950s one of our party returned from a hunting sortie and told of a sable bull that he had wounded. A trip the following day to obtain additional licences to hunt zebra had delayed tracking down the wounded sable. I knew enough about the ethics of big game hunting to realise this was an unsportsmanlike attitude, and I asked whether he had any objection to my going out to try to finish the animal off? No, he said, he didn't mind in the least, and even offered me his tracker to aid in the search. I set off with his tracker and my own in search of the wounded sable.

Sable bull

We had been walking for some five hours when we came into an open, grassy glade with mopane trees on the slopes on both sides. I recall the scene quite vividly; I was eating raisins from a stock in my pocket as the two trackers cast around looking for tracks. Suddenly, there he was – a coal-black sable bull facing me not twenty yards away. He snorted and took off. The trackers shouted out that this was indeed the wounded sable we were looking for and off we sped after him. He ran into the mopane woodland and after a chase of about five minutes we halted, out of breath, on the top of a slope. Then we saw him again, below us this time, looking back to where he thought we must be.

I took a dead rest on the shoulder of one tracker and fired, shattering the sable's left front leg. He pitched forward, then got up and scrambled down the loose rock, his leg dangling uselessly. One tracker, an ex-mine police guard, went after the animal with an axe to finish him off. Then the magnificent creature turned, offering his final defiance, on three legs and with a nasty wound in his stomach. I took careful aim and dropped him.

I put down my rifle and gazed down at this dying animal. What, I asked myself, was I doing? Why had I trekked all this way to find an animal wounded by someone else who lacked the elementary sportmanship of finishing it off himself?

We had caused this creature unbelievable agony and for what?

The final irony came later. We returned to camp carrying the skin and horns of the antelope and one shoulder of meat. It had been a hard, slogging day, but at least we had something to show for it. In the evening, when the others returned to the camp and heard my story, the man who had first wounded the sable promptly laid claim to the trophy. It was his, he insisted, because he had first wounded the animal. I was stunned. The other man, however, disputed his claim and awarded me the trophy. Did I want it, I wondered?

No other mutual venture, I believe, can trigger off and expose one's strengths and weaknesses more than a spell in the bush when hunting is the objective. The best can be a trusted companion at your side, someone whose presence could make the difference between life and death or serious injury; and around the campfire, hunters tend to talk freely and bonds of lasting comradeship can be forged. The worst is when miserable attitudes emerge in people you never suspected capable of such failings.

Looking back, I must affirm that my experience in hunting has been of considerable benefit to my career as a conservationist. It taught me as much about human behaviour as about animals. It taught me about tracking and enabled me to read and understand the signs of the wild. In later years, my attitude to hunting has matured to the point where I can appreciate that it plays a useful part in game conservation. License fees help fund wildlife agencies, and sport hunting promotes keeping of wildlife on private lands. I can accept that culling in national parks is vital to wildlife management and survival of populations.

But modern hunting is demonstrably so easy that it is no longer a sport in the accepted meaning of the word. On an organised safari in which the guide leads you to the animal you are after and steps back to allow you to administer the *coup de grace*, no elephant, or lion, or buffalo, or any other species of game has a sporting chance.

It *was* different in the old days, though only to a degree. You had to find your own quarry, track it, sometimes for days and on foot, and shoot it with an open-sight gun that was by no means foolproof. Then, the danger was real and, in many cases, hunters paid with life or limb for pitting themselves against creatures stronger and faster and with a lot more stamina.

However, people have always won out in the end. We have a better brain than the beasts of the plains or forests and that is what counts. We can out-think our quarry, we can fashion weapons. Even a primitive spear or arrow, poisoned dart, or slingshot are too much for four-footed creatures. Consider the Bushmen of the Kalahari, to appreciate what a skilled human hunter can do against any animal, no matter how dangerous – and no matter how flimsy the weapons at the hunter's disposal.

But, for all that, I am careful not to adopt a righteous attitude towards hunters. Those of old may have hunted with disregard for the numbers they killed, but they left a lot of their knowledge of the wild behind in their writings and their diaries and they simply knew no better; ecology and conservation were unknown terms to Selous and Gordon-Cumming. They killed under the impression that there was unlimited game in the bush. It seemed so at the time. What difference could one more dead animal make?

Being a game ranger turned out to have limitations, too. Early in 1967, since it was plainly impossible to support my new wife on my meagre ranger's salary, I returned to Johannesburg. A flat in a Hillbrow high-rise was something of a shock after wide open Botswana. I concentrated on animal paintings (on the dining room table). Still unable to afford oils and canvas, I stayed with the wash technique – Indian ink and water on paper – and began to earn a living in the

advertising department of the Herbert Evans paint manufacturing company. One especially pleasant duty was to run the Herbert Evans art gallery, an institution which grew in size and prestige over the years until it was closed when the company was sold.

I took every opportunity of going out into the bush; I joined one or two hunting expeditions, and began to visit the Kruger National Park, Zululand, and the Northern Transvaal taking photographs. Mozambique was still open to visitors, and I went several times to the vast and haunting expanses of Namibia. Then a friend, Johannesburg fashion entrepreneur Michael Brett, invited me to join him on a wilderness trail in the Umfolozi Game Reserve in Natal, where Ian Player ran the Wilderness Leadership School trailing operation. The trail officer was Don Richards, our guide and teacher for the next five days.

By then I imagined I knew a good deal about everything concerned with wildlife. I knew a bit about firearms, I thought I knew about hunting and game-ranging, I was making good headway as a wildlife artist, and had every reason, as I thought, to be pleased with the way my life was shaping up. But it was in 1971, at Umfolozi, on a wilderness trail, that I realised how much I still had to learn.

Don Richards was an excellent environmental educator. It was through his inspiration on that five-day trail at the Umfolozi Game Reserve and at Lake St Lucia that the light, so to speak, went on for me. For the first time, it seemed, I became really aware of plant life, what fresh water was, what pollution meant, and what walking in the bush felt like. It was a spiritual experience; I can put in no other way. It transformed me. It was like nothing else that had ever happened to me – not art, photography, flying, or being a game ranger.

Walking on that wilderness trail in the company of Don Richards, I resolved that I had to embark upon this most rewarding field. The idea began to form of running trails specifically tailored for young people – school children. Conita was enthusiastic, and we began to look for support to get the venture going.

In 1972, we found it. Together with a Johannesburg medical man, Dr. Jean-Jacques Brossi, and a local dentist, Dr. Eric Thorburn, we launched our first wilderness trail operation, on a part-time, non-profit basis. I count myself fortunate to have found partners who have supported my enthusiasms, and this was a prime example. The time had come for my second chance at a wildlife career, working simultaneously at wildlife painting and conservation education. I joined Ian

Player's organisation and served on the Transvaal side of his Wilderness Leadership School, running trails and promoting wilderness awareness, and also began taking parties of schoolboys and adults to the Tuli Block on trailing expeditions which proved an outstanding success.

The youngsters were intrigued with the mysteries of the wild. Children make the most appreciative audiences of all for new experiences. Not for them the boredom, indifference or practised cynicism to be found among some adults. The greatest thrill was to see the sudden awakening of enthusiasm for a subject which lends itself so immediately to a spirit of dedication. Time and again, I have witnessed the dawning in teenage eyes of an inspirational awareness that here was a field to which one could devote one's life and talents.

Trailing means walking in wild country. It can be in the Fish River Canyon, along the Otter Trail, or anywhere else with enough wild space to lose yourself, and be free for a while from human artifice. The kind of trailing I have concentrated on has been wilderness trailing in big game country.

But trailing means specifically *walking*, whether carrying a backpack or carrying no more than a sun hat. It emphatically does not mean driving along in an open Land Rover with a pair of binoculars slung around one's neck. When you are

martial eagle.
a/.

walking, your entire surroundings are accessible to eye, ear and nose. In our case, it meant walking, between one base and another, through country where encounters with potentially dangerous animals were a possibility.

It has always been our declared aim to acquaint people better with their wild environment, to get them excited about nature in a way which would not otherwise be possible. Our experience has been that men and women who undertake to trudge through the bush well away from any built-up areas develop their own affinity with the wild. There is something about a wilderness trail that opens a window into our soul, and there are few trailists who will not testify to its magic. For many it is an emotional happening, the birth of a feeling which stays with them for the rest of their lives and often compels them to return again and again.

The following year, I was fortunate enough to be among the artists invited to visit the United States to attend a hunters' convention held by Game Conservation International in San Antonio, Texas. Ian Player was there, as was Barry Clements, director of the Wilderness Leadership School. I exhibited eight or nine pictures and sold most of them, but the highlight of being there was meeting renowned British wildlife artist David Shepherd, whose work had also been on display, along with that of other distinguished American and European artists.

David had painted a picture entitled "Tiger Fire", a magnificent representation of a Bengal tiger. In association with the World Wildlife Fund, he had published 850 prints of this painting which sold for one hundred dollars each. This raised a considerable amount of money for the Fund's Operation Tiger, a campaign to save that beautiful animal from total extinction. It sparked off an idea in my head. Why not try something along the same lines?

On my return I set about painting a watercolour of a pair of cheetah, since these animals were at the time a focus of concern about endangered species. With the help of Johannesburg businessman Neville Anderson, I had it published in an edition of 250, and we sold the entire edition within a month.

Then, at a wildlife management symposium in Pretoria, I found myself seated next to Professor Koos Bothma of the University of Pretoria, and told Prof. Bothma I had raised six thousand rand through my picture, and would the university like to use the money for a survey of what was happening to the cheetah in South Africa? Prof. Bothma quickly agreed. To formalize the arrangements, we needed an institution responsible for maintaining a watchful eye on animals in southern Africa facing extinction, to monitor their progress, and to provide funds as and when needed to press for additional conservation measures. The notion of the Endangered Wildlife Trust was born. With the aid of Neville Anderson and a lawyer friend, Dawie Botha, who undertook the legal requirements, and with an investment of five hundred rand of my own, the Endangered Wildlife Trust was formed with Neville, James Clarke of the *Star*, and me as the trustees. The three of us ran the Trust for some three years on our own.

I would like to think that my next idea for fundraising for the Trust in South Africa was original and rewarding. What I did was approach several well-known South African artists – Leigh Voight, Paul Rose, Vic Andrews, Dino Paravano, Vic Guhrs, Keith Joubert, Paul Bosman, Kim Donaldson, Ingred Weisby – and persuade each to donate a painting. Several hundred numbered prints were run off and sold, and one lucky purchaser was drawn as the winner of the original work. In this fashion, enough revenue was generated to keep the work of the Trust expanding. The system also had the effect of instilling wide interest and enrolling members for the EWT from among those who purchased paintings. My work now went almost entirely into funding the EWT and raised some R100 000 over the next ten years.

The Endangered Wildlife Trust remained linked to the Eugene Marais Chair of Wildlife Management at Pretoria University. I became the first EWT chairman in an honorary capacity. Seven years later in 1980, I stepped down as chairman to become director, a position I held until 1985, when I left because the Lapalala Wilderness School – a long-standing dream of mine – was opening. By then, the Trust had become an important body governed by a board of leading businesspeople and academics. Ken Whyte took over from me as chairman and played a major role in directing the affairs of the Trust.

The Trust had done and continues to do extremely valuable work. It stimulates public awareness of endangered species, carries out surveys and research, and financially supports special ventures such as the Vulture Study Group (initially via John Ledger, who subsequently became EWT director) by providing funds which enable them to survive and thrive. It has undertaken research on the brown hyaena and cheetah – the cheetah spoor remains the emblem of the Trust; has carried out projects on rhino and elephant; monitored the ivory trade; equipped many research projects with hardware such as radio tracking gear; and has assisted students financially and in many other ways. It is today an organisation which is recognised and respected internationally.

field sketch of
young Kudo bull.

The international reputation of the Trust provided me with opportunities to travel and lecture in Kenya, India, Sri Lanka, Israel, the United States, Canada, South America, Britain and a number of European countries, as well as travelling extensively throughout southern Africa in the execution of Trust work.

That gives you the chronology. But life can't always be represented very well as a linear affair. Often the circles count for more. In 1975 – our earlier trailing endeavour having ended because of conflict with landowners and other difficulties, Mike Brett entered the picture again and assisted Conita and me in setting up our own full-time wildlife trailing operation: Educational Wildlife Expeditions. He supplied the office and vehicle to get us started and Educational Wildlife Expeditions came into being as a non-profit venture, registered as such, eventually employing a total of ten officers in Johannesburg and Botswana. Mike pulled out when he departed for the United States and Val Ford took his place. Over more than fifteen years, we have taken literally thousands of people into the bush, mainly in Botswana.

Meanwhile, Don Richards left the Wilderness Leadership School to launch the aforementioned environmental education program at Treverton, and after some years left Treverton to join our

Lapalala Wilderness School educational staff.
In another satisfying circle, for the fifteenth
anniversary of the Endangered Wildlife Trust in
1988, the same David Shepherd whose tiger
painting inspired that first EWT cheetah fundraiser donated a painting, of which limited edition prints raised some R300 000 for the Trust's
and Rhino and Elephant Foundation's conservation work.

In 1956 I thought hunting safaris could satisfy my
yen for the bush. By 1966 I thought game-ranging
could do it, but in 1971 in Umfolozi I realised
that trailing worked better, because of its impact
on other people. Now, looking back on EWT's
early years of devotion to the cheetah, it occurs
to me that we may very well have been wasting
valuable time. Saving the cheetah is not conservation in the true meaning of the word: it's just a
small part of the process. We need to care
about cheetahs and elephants because if we

don't, we are but a short step from relinquishing
concern about each other. Who cares about the
Ethiopians? Who gives a damn if all the Afghan
rebels are terminated? Why worry at all about
the ravages of war or famine or pestilence or
pollution?

The threads have come together. The real empha-
sis in wildlife conservation and at EWT these
days is on getting people to understand the
importance and value of nature to the human
world, not just who is killing sable, or cheetahs,
or elephants. This also is the aim of trailing – to
draw people out of urban offices into a wild
world of which they may have been only dimly
aware. Having people grasp what it is that must
be conserved is far and away the most crucial
part of the task. Conservation is a stony road, pit-
ted with ignorance and indifference. But once
people become both aware and concerned, the
battle of the environment enters a new phase.

6.
Tuli, River of Dust

If you ask people about Tuli, and they know anything about the place at all, chances are they will soon mention elephants. As the twentieth century moves to a close, there remains just one free-ranging, flourishing elephant population on private land south of the Zambezi River – the elephants of Botswana's Tuli Block.

Even if you'd never heard of the Tuli elephants, upon arriving in the area you'd soon realise something was wrong. Although the Tuli is today characterised by private game reserves, much of the country looks denuded – where is the tall grass? What has been breaking and stripping the trees? It wouldn't take long even for a novice to guess that elephant numbers are considerable. But it wasn't always so.

The first white man known to have hunted elephant on the Limpopo was the renegade Coenraad de Buys in 1809. Records are scanty but he appears to have been a fearless hunter, despatching elephant at close quarters with an ancient muzzleloader. He was followed by trader-explorers such as David Hulme, who penetrated as far as the Shashe River. At a Grahamstown sale one year, Hulme sold 2 333 pounds of ivory for £5 259. This represented more than 250 elephants. In their northward movement, the Transvaal Boers were not slow to dispose of elephants either. Petrus Jacobs brought down two hundred elephants on one expedition alone.

antlion larva

Between 1846 and 1848 there entered on the scene a man who was to leave his mark firmly on the southern African scene, Roualeyn Gordon-Cumming. Eton-educated, he was the second son of a Scottish baronet, and reportedly went about the bush in a kind of kilt. He conducted two expeditions into the Tuli area, hunting between the Shoshong and Motloutse rivers and along the Limpopo.

"We resumed the spoor at a rapid pace," he relates of one incident, "and presently on my left I heard the joyous signal 'Klaw' (Tswana for elephant; the accepted spelling is *tlou*), and cantering in that direction I came full in sight of an enormous bull elephant marching along at a free majestic pace and in another minute I was riding by his side. I fired thirteen bullets at his head and shoulders, he made a rapid charge and disappeared among the trees. Cautiously following I discovered him lying in an upright position with his two forelegs stretched out before him. Fancying he was still alive, I fired both barrels at his ear but though the balls rang loudly on his venerable head, the noble elephant heeded not the force, his ancient spirit had departed."

Following in the wake of hunters were traders, who swapped guns for ivory with African chiefs and headmen. What the tribesmen lacked in shooting skill they made up for in patience,

bushcraft, and thorough understanding of game. By 1855 elephants were so scarce in the Tuli area that hunters such as Baldwin, Oswell, Finaughty and Selous had to venture much further north. By the time Selous led the Pioneer Column into Mashonaland in July 1890, the country was empty of elephant. From the Motloutse to the Shashe no elephants were to be observed for the next fifty years.

The territory from which the elephants had been driven became the subject of negotiations between Cecil John Rhodes and Khama the Great. Rhodes, dreaming of his Cape to Cairo railway, persuaded Khama to grant him rights to the huge chunk of land now called the Tuli Block, on one condition: that the area be divided into farms and settled. (Khama's concession included the 40 000 hectares lying to the west of Shashe River, today known as the Tuli Circle and in use as a controlled hunting area administered by the Zimbabwe Department of National Parks and Wildlife Conservation.)

Although elephants were not seen in the Tuli area for so many decades, they had not disappeared forever. In the 1940s a certain Dr. Nel of Pietersburg became the first Tuli landowner to sight the return of the huge animals. Elephants began to move in steadily from the north and west from that time. By 1956 Bechuanaland had established a game department which, like many other similar departments, was formed in order to control elephants in tribal and irrigation areas, an operation that eventually accounted for the death of 1 800 elephants. Bechuanaland's policy was to control the elephants east of the railway line, containing them in areas to which the tribesmen would consent.

What started the big movement of elephants into this corner of Botswana? Rhodesia had started to control elephants on tribal lands, while Transvaal farmers owning land along the Limpopo were reportedly shooting indiscriminately. Once more hounded by the gun and diminishing habitat, the elephant began retreating into the Tuli enclave – there was nowhere else for them to go.

In 1960 one Tuli landowner counted three hundred elephants. By the seventies there were reports of a vast increase in elephant numbers and widespread habitat destruction. Cries for

reduction of elephants began to be heard. Fears increased with the proposed erection of a veterinary fence from the Shashe to the Motloutse. Large numbers of elephant moving west would cause tremendous damage to such a fence. But did the elephants move west? And what was the importance of the movement?

March 1976 found me in the office of Botswana's Department of Wildlife and National Parks. The result of my visit was a report emphasising that before a sound management policy could be established, information was needed on population and movements throughout the range; and that research should begin with aerial counts. The Botswana game department supported these findings, as did the Tuli landowners, who had combined into the Eastern Tuli Game Protection Association for the common purpose of creating a sanctuary. The first aerial count commenced in June 1976, funded by the Endangered Wildlife Trust and Educational Wildlife Expeditions, and revealed forty-three elephants. The Wildlife

Society of Southern Africa and the Wilderness Trust contributed to a count four months later, on which I accompanied Larry Patterson, ecologist with the Botswana Department of Wildlife and National Parks. We counted 590 elephants from the air. Although we flew east to cover the Tuli Circle in this survey, we saw no sign of elephant there.

Larry, Dave Peacock and I carried out a third survey, this time counting only 190 elephants. We saw plenty of elephant spoor in the mud in the Tuli Circle, but again no elephant. Had they gone to the west with the onset of the rainy season, we wondered? No one knew.

On February 21, 1977 we had a mishap with the Department of Wildlife Maule Rocket when landing at Safari Ranch to borrow a fuel pump. Larry, who was flying the aircraft, came in to land with the tail too high and the propellor struck the

Ground hornbill
GW.

ground, but we didn't realise there had been damage until we took off for Pont Drift and had difficulty in gaining altitude. It was only that afternoon as Larry did his checks in preparation for a three-hour survey flight that he discovered the prop bent somewhat back around the cowling, and promptly called off the survey.

The reason for concern about the elephants was simple: increasing numbers and diminishing range. Erection of a veterinary fence would reduce this range further. We already knew from our wilderness trails that these elephants were touchy, and capable of being very nasty because of the human harassment they had suffered, not only from shooting but also in recent years by over-enthusiastic game rangers wishing to give clients excitement and better photographic opportunities. Underlying that concern was the question of the long-term conservation of the area. Tuli may translate as "river of dust," but that wasn't a good enough reason to allow elephants to damage irretrievably the superb riverine habitat along the courses of the three great rivers – the Motloutse in the west, the Shashe in the east, and the Limpopo forming the southern boundary of their new home range. It would be too much of an irony for the renewed elephant boom after the years of bust to result in plunder of the very habitat that had supplied them with sanctuary.

Adrian Boshier, if he were alive, would agree with those sentiments. Ted Steyn, the father of what has become the Mashatu game reserve, certainly did too. He believed in the establishment of a permanent sanctuary and worked tirelessly to achieve that objective. In 1978 the most pressing need appreared to be obtaining data on elephant numbers and habitats, and this was the impulse for the EWT becoming involved in a joint research project under Professor Brian Walker of the University of the Witwatersrand. The Tuli elephants were not an endangered species; they were the focal point for drawing attention to the threatened habitat.

We planned an ecological study of the Tuli enclave, and a marking programme with the object of collaring twenty elephants – five bulls and fifteen cows – which we hoped would enable researcher Bruce Page to keep track of them. We had our fair share of excitement during the marking programme and nearly lost two assistants in the process.

At the commencement of the project we had with us Eric Thorburn, a trustee of the EWT, who planned to film the darting with a view to producing a half-hour film which we could use to raise further funds. Eric also planned as an experiment to mark the ivory by acid etching. Our first elephant was a large cow which Larry darted

from a Hughes 300 piloted by a young Swiss woman, Pirot Peroz. Everything went according to plan. The tusks were marked and a collar fitted in good time. Unfortunately, as often happened before darting became fairly routine, we wound up with far too many people in attendance. Our elephant cow got up quickly after receiving the antidote and we believed she would amble off. She chose otherwise, however, and charged straight at the nearest people, who happened to be Eric and me. I shouted to Eric, who was laden with equipment, to run and in spite of his impediment he took off at high speed. The person protecting us, together with the rest of the team, had disappeared in the confusion.

I barely had time to yell at Eric and then take off myself, and it was only a chance distraction that caused the cow to change direction suddenly and leave the now fleeing Eric to his own private hell. She probably would have killed him if she could have laid her trunk upon his neck. The shock was considerable. He subsequently lost a good deal of weight and his nerves were shattered. All of us involved had a very serious talk that evening, and resolved to ensure that greater care was taken in future.

The week of darting progressed without further incident until we darted a large bull in the Shashe riverine bush opposite the Zimbabwe

`tsetse`

border. This bull refused to rise after the antidote. Even when coaxed with the assistance of a large rope attached to a tusk, he still lay flat on the ground. We were growing concerned – the temperature was rising as the morning progressed.

Larry finally went up and gave the bull a good few sharp slaps and yelled at him, which elicited instantaneous reaction. The bull rose rapidly before us, but because of our consternation over his failure to respond to the antidote, we had at that point taken no precautions. One vehicle was parked facing the elephant. Here Koos Bothma and I took refuge, Koos diving into the open back and I into the cab.

The rest of the party took off on the run, not always easy over chewed up ilala palms, which can have the effect of slipping out from under you like a loose rug. Most made it to the nearest trees. One supremely successful attempt to climb was by our senior scout, who leaped onto and clean over the backs of the other terrified souls and was soon at the top of a tree.

Derek Ritchie, in charge of collars, had the closest call. Derek is one of those amazing people who, inspite of a physical handicap, has tackled life with verve and shrinks from nothing. His task was to attach the nine-ton breaking strain collars around the necks of immobilised elephants. But he was not able to get around as quickly as we could. He lost his balance in the retreat and ended up on the ground in front of the elephant bull. There was not much he could do except remain perfectly still, which under the circumstances was the most sensible thing to do.

The elephant, for all that was going on around him, stood there with the rope dangling from his tusk and made no move for at least a minute. We stared at him, not knowing what he would do. At last, to our incredulous relief, he wheeled and disappeared into the dense undergrowth, rope still attached. Derek had another unfortunate episode when we were marking elephants in the Klaserie game reserve, adjacent to the Kruger National Park, in a project similar to that in Tuli. That time the veterinarian was Eddie Young, then working with the Transvaal Division of Nature Conservation. A fairly big bull had been darted near the Klaserie River and had crossed over a stretch of deep water into a narrow gulley. Had the drug acted more swiftly, the bull could have gone down in the river and drowned. He wasted no time in getting the ground team to him. Loaded down with two heavy collars, plus bits and pieces of equipment, Derek plunged into the river, believing it to be shallow enough to be forded on foot. Alas, the spot he chose was deep and the next instant he disappeared, preceded by a yell. The weight of the collars added to his difficulties and he had to be hauled out, swearing profusely but otherwise intact.

"It is not easy," wrote Ian Parker in his book *Ivory Crisis*, "to look back on what one has done and admit that much, if not most, was futile. The only salve to conscience and ego is if at the time one acted, it was in the belief that one was right."

In the case of Tuli we never obtained the required ecological data, and the area still is not under unified management as a permanent sanctuary, dear Elephant, Sir, although law enforcement is more effective today than it once was. The elephants wander across an area of more than 850 square kilometres of unfenced country belonging to fourteen landowners, and Tuli is little closer to understanding its elephant population.

Some things bear mention, however. The years of ivory hunting and poaching seem to have resulted in generic selection against big ivory. These animals mainly carry small ivory or none – too few big-ivory genes persisted, perhaps. The elephants are much more inclined to be jumpy and skittish about people than Kruger Park elephants, for example. Elephants live a long time; these apparently still carry clan memories of persecution. And they are in the distinctive position of being too numerous for their range when elephants have been decimated in so many other places. The River of Dust notwithstanding, long may their boom continue.

Tree breaker

7.
The Ivory Trail

My wilderness trail party had stopped for a lunchbreak under a large mashatu tree. We had put on the kettle and set out the cheese, biscuits and tinned fish. Cameras had been laid aside, and with a superb feeling of total relaxation we had spread ourselves out under the branches.

Then game scout Johannes Naari announced that an elephant was bearing down on us. She had not one, but two calves of different sizes with her. Apparently unaware of us, she was heading straight for our tree. We leapt into action, some climbing the great tree and others pressing ourselves close against its trunk. (If you have ever climbed a smooth wall, you know what it is like to climb a mashatu tree.) Tea was knocked into the fire, cameras ground carelessly into the sand. At our commotion the elephant came to halt three metres from the outermost branches. She rose up very tall, and with curved back and outstretched tail stalked rapidly past the tree. Then, protecting the calves on her outer flank, she turned and retreated the way she had come, leaving us with a clearer image than any of us wanted of the pink around her eyes.

Breathing more easily later, I remembered what Captain J.F. Elton, Her Majesty's Consul in Mozambique and evidently aware of what a burden professional dignity can be, had written in 1879:

yellowbilled hornbill

"Being charged by an elephant is a new sensation – very absorbing for the time, and it would be excellent relaxation once a week – say every Saturday afternoon, for overworked men in high office." My trailists were all men in high office — members of the Johannesburg City Council!

When I returned to the Tuli Block in 1975 I already knew the elephants well from encounters with them at close quarters on foot ten years before as a ranger. Having formed Educational Wildlife Expeditions to help open the minds of as many people as possible to wilderness, we were drawn irresistably back to Tuli. And because of the elephants, we called this the Ivory Trail, after the title of the book by T. V. Bulpin about the ivory hunter Cecil "Bvekenya" Barnard's exploits not far to the east.

Tuli was ideal for the Ivory Trail, and few trails in southern Africa could match the sheer splendour of that wild country. Walking among hundreds of elephants is an experience never to be forgotten, and Tuli has hundreds of elephants. They move, most often, in large groups and one needs all one's wits about one. The skill of an experienced tracker is essential. I was fortunate in having two such men, both born in the Tuli Block. Johannes Naari had worked with me since 1966 and was very steady even under considerable pressure. Johannes Phetou was excellent up to the point of contact with a grey friend, although he then retreated to the back of the line. Before setting off on a trail I would call the group together and brief them on what to expect, what to do, and what not to do. But the best laid plans can go awry.

Trying to keep six people atop a double antheap calm when more than a hundred elephants are slowly approaching, for example, is not to be recommended for the faint-hearted. I did not feel too good, as I had imagined that the animals would pass to one side, giving us a grand view, but instead they looked as though they were going to surround us. Growing through the double antheap was a sturdy intertwining shrub and here we now crouched down. The terrain was open on both sides, punctuated only by occasional haak-en-steek acacias, not ideal for climbing.

By the time I realised the precarious nature of our position there was nothing to do but sit tight. I hoped neither of the girls in the party would faint or scream. An enormous cow followed by her family came steadily closer and seemed intent on feeding on our shrub. Johannes Naari was up in front of me and facing her, while my trail group members made themselves as small as possible. Soon elephants were on both sides of our antheap and the tension was unbelievable.

At Johannes's whispered suggestion, I took out my hunting knife and began digging away at the antheap for sand clods. Clutching my rifle, perspiration running down past my ears and eyes, I almost fell off the antheap. By this stage the leading elephant was but a few metres away and Johannes hurled a well-directed clod, which hit her on the ear. She was so close that we could see every vein in her ear as she brought her trunk up to touch the spot. Another clod caught her on the trunk and a well-aimed shot hit a younger elephant coming up alongside her.

Now I too started to cast a few clods at the wall of at least ten elephants standing in front of us. Incredibly, they seemed to have no idea we were there, presumably not having smelled us. They just appeared mystified at the painless missiles raining down on them. The big cow backed off, bumping into an elephant behind her, and started to turn. There was no sound from the elephants whatsoever. With back arched and large ears held forward, she strode off and the rest followed suit. They could not have been closer. The trailists tumbled off the antheap in nervous relief, and had no further desire to see any elephant at close range for a while.

Not all encounters have such happy endings. While elephant normally display a gentle manner, they are also capable of immense fury. Some tourists (not trailists) on safari in the Transvaal Lowveld a few years ago went after a group of cows and calves on foot, leaving their vehicle on the side of the track. Exactly what happened cannot be known, but their walk ended in tragedy with the death of a young woman.

The group had followed the elephants into thick bush and had come up to a large antheap. The tourists were not very well concealed when a young elephant spotted them and trumpeted shrilly, causing its mother to come running to its aid. At this point, fear and confusion apparently sent the party running away down a track away from the elephant. The young ranger ran across the elephant's bows trying to distract her, but to no avail. The cow tore after the fleeing tourists. Last in line was a young mother of two, who was rapidly overtaken.

From accounts, she screamed once before the cow struck her a violent blow across her back, breaking her neck instantly. The force flung her through the air and she landed up against some low bushes, where the furious cow pulverised the woman with her forehead. A number of elephant had followed her in a highly nervous state, and when the cow had spent her fury they all disappeared into the surrounding bush. I visited the spot a few days later with the warden of the reserve, who recounted the tragedy for me, and I

later was called to give evidence in court because a charge of manslaughter was laid against the ranger in charge.

Johannes Naari learned something of elephant retaliation as a boy of fourteen when his father went out to the mealie lands one night, loudly beating a paraffin tin to drive out elephants. Returning later, Johannes's father was confronted by the looming shape of an angry elephant, which chased him, tusking him in the side. When he did not return, his family went out to search for him, and found him face down in a critical state. He died from the wounds he had received later that night.

Johannes was luckier when he took a corner in his Land Rover and encountered a baby elephant right in the road. The mother, slightly hidden in the bush nearby, immediately made for Johannes in a determined fashion, and he shot off the track at speed with the cow running alongside. The Land Rover was completely open and Johannes had to duck his head to avoid thorny branches whipping by while also trying to watch his direction and keep an eye on the angry cow. He engaged a rather large leadwood tree, and, apparently satisfied, the cow and calf then departed, leaving a dazed and extremely relieved Johannes and a Land Rover with a crushed mudguard.

A game scout named Jeremiah, from Tuli's Charter reserve had a different elephant-vehicle experience. He was riding home from the trading store in a donkey cart, accompanied by his wife and Boetie, his brother, when an onrushing, trumpeting elephant set his donkeys and cart into rapid motion. They came to a most positive halt when the cart lodged one wheel in an aardvark hole. The bull elephant rushed by, making a terrible noise and slashing his head from side to side. Jeremiah leapt off the cart and crawled into an ilala thicket, leaving his wife and Boetie prostrate on the cart floor. The donkeys remained motionless, heads down. The elephant backed off, charged twice more, and then abandoned the venture. Soon after, Jeremiah resigned his post and became a barman at a game lodge.

I once fled for my life along with some trailists when we disturbed a group of cows and calves that pursued us with great ferocity. Although armed, I had no mind to harm them. Killing a cow elephant means trauma for the whole family unit and causes great disruption. That day I had led my trail group into broken mopane woodland, having seen a group of elephant from a low ridge. What caused them to turn on us I did not wait to find out. They were routinely harassed by rangers driving tourists around the bush and crashing too closely after any elephant they chanced upon; this may have been the reason for

Being charged by an elephant is a new sensation

their charging us, combined with the fact that cows are so protective of their young.

The sound of breaking branches and clattering stones heralded their arrival. I shouted to Johannes to take off. He needed no second urging and together with John Farrant, one of my party, led a blind rush away down a rock gulley. Too many lunches and too little exercise made little perceptible difference as the trailists – some decidedly overweight – sped over the rough ground. The trumpeting of the herd chilled us with fear. And then, as quickly as it had started, so it ended. The elephants turned away.

That's how it is with elephant encounters – usually serene, sometimes alarming, sometimes lethal, always impressive. That was the legacy of the Ivory Trail. Even once back in the office again, participants felt they had come to know something of elephants as the essence of wilderness. People who have met elephants up close are never quite the same again. The animals' size alone accounts for part of this – what is it in us that makes us respond to simple bigness? Their awesome power, although rarely witnessed, is somehow understood nevertheless. And while one may feel that zebras or impala, for instance, are operating mainly on knee-jerk instinctive impulses, with elephants it's difficult to shake off the idea that they are *thinking*.

8.
Tiger Fire

As we were thrusting through the tall grass in search of the one-horned rhino in Chitwan, we were joined by another elephant, a bull with splendid tusks and very tall. The name of the newcomer was Shamshahar and we learned that he was noted for a long-ago moment of weakness, despite his impressive appearance.

Land Rovers for game viewing are out of the question in Chitwan National Park owing to the dense jungle terrain and high grass – you need some height for clear viewing. Those same factors mean walking isn't ideal. It is not like walking in the African bush where visibility is generally good, although facing a black rhino on foot is certainly more dangerous than confronting a one-horned Asian rhino. The presence of tigers and sloth bears also make game viewing on foot impractical here. So trained elephants provide the transportation and visitors have the exotic experience of viewing wildlife from a wonderfully elevated – and elevating – perspective.

Once K. K. Gurung, former manager of the famous Tiger Tops jungle lodge, had to use Shamshahar and four other elephants from the herd at Tiger Tops to recover the body of a villager who had been killed by a tiger. They found the tiger before they found the poor villager and the cat immediately came at the advancing elephants with a roar.

Under the command of their mahouts, the four elephant females stood their ground, trembling. Not so Shamshahar. He about-turned and tore through the jungle with some very anxious passengers trying desperately to cling to their wildly rocking howdah. When we met Shamshahar he appeared not to have suffered lasting psychic damage from the incident. Or perhaps he knew from the routine that this time we were looking for rhino and not tiger.

I had once ridden an Asian elephant – we then called them Indian elephants – at the age of six in the Johannesburg Zoo. But this was altogether another kind of proposition. The mahouts drive the elephants through the tall grass seeking rhino regularly twice a day, and the elephants show no fear of the rhino. In some areas the elephant grass has been cut down in lines about fifty metres wide and here one is able to observe the rhino with greater ease. To the purist this may seem artificial, but given the nature of the terrain and the number of people who visit Chitwan, the grass cutting is a practical convenience.

Upon sighting a rhino the mahout whistles up his colleagues who immediately turn their elephants toward his call. Very gently, the rhino is cornered. Care is exercised for the rhino have been known to charge, but this is fortunately a rare occurrence.

I've always been a dreamer, but dreams do come true if you dream often enough. I saw my first Siberian tiger in the huge cat section of the Bronx Zoo in New York behind steel, glass and concrete on a clear day in May of 1973. My wife and I had ridden the subway from Manhattan to the Bronx, itself an experience. The subway trains with their graffiti and hungry, desperate people felt far more dangerous than the Indian jungle.

On the side of the tiger's cage we read that his breed was the world's largest cat, and that there were only 150 left in their native wilds; it read on that there were three hundred known Rembrandt paintings and the last had sold in New York for a million dollars. "How much do you think a Siberian tiger is worth?" concluded the sign. I never forgot that. It spurred me on to seeing a tiger in the wild one day.

So it was that eleven years later in November 1984 I did finally visit India and Nepal. My young son Anton and I were with the Endangered Wildlife Trust Explorers Club on an expedition to South-east Asia and I was the leader of a group of eighteen people.

Four in the morning found us aboard our Air Mauritius jet liner approaching Bombay, city of nine million people, on the west coast of India, not without some apprehension. India's Prime

Minister, Indira Ghandi, had been assassinated a week earlier and India was in turmoil. We suffered more apprehension after we landed, for we had never imagined that so many people could squeeze into an airport terminal at that early hour of the morning. After a short wait for customs and immigration formalities, we found ourselves in the main hall under the care of our local agent. No one dared to leave luggage, for if one was so rash as to give it to a willing helper to carry out to the waiting bus, luggage and porter might never be seen again.

As our bus drove into Bombay we saw hundreds of white-linen-clad figures lying in doorways, on benches, on the beaches and on the pavements. Children defecated on the pavements as their mothers drew up water from nearby wells. There were multitudes of beggars and a sea of humanity which surpassed anything I had ever seen. Modern India. How could this country of poverty and malnutrition have achieved so much in conservation of wildlife? We were struck with the enormity of it all.

We arrived in Delhi a few days later and, sadly, were advised that our journey to Corbett Tiger Sanctuary had been cancelled. Numerous people had been murdered on the road to Corbett from Delhi, and fairly close to the city we had our first taste of the malaise in the aftermath of the slay-

ing of Prime Minister Ghandi. Our course was altered and we headed for Jaipur, city of the ancient Moguls, then on to the Sariska Tiger Sanctuary. Jaipur is straight out of the fifteenth century and there my son and I rode an elephant up the long incline leading to the walled Amber Palace. I marvelled at the elephants' pace and the way they fit into modern India.

Bullocks pulling cart
with grass.
jaipur. India 84.

Besides elephants, the Indians also use three-wheeled black and yellow scooters and one night we were treated to a race at breakneck speed downtown. Those who have seen the movie *Octopussy*, starring Roger Moore as 007, may recall a high-speed chase through the streets of Jaipur. We spent our time dodging various vehicles, cows and the odd elephant. Better to hit a pedestrian or an elephant than a sacred cow – to this the driver paid particular attention.

Jaipur is in the arid state of Rajasthan, where the heat rose up to suffocate us like a blanket over our heads. We were eager to strike out for Sariska in the hope of catching a glimpse of a tiger and spending a few relaxing days in the Indian jungle. Two things complicated our quest, however. Firstly, many of our group had gone down with Delhi belly, which is guaranteed to put you off looking for tigers. Our journey was frequently halted by cries to stop the bus and some poor member of the group would hurtle off the bus into the thick vegetation lining the roadway, sometimes startling the odd pig or Egyptian vulture. Known as scavenger vultures in India, the birds are far from extinct and thank goodness for that, because without them and the pigs the country would have even more serious health problems than it does. The Collins guide to the birds of India describes the vulture thus: "It is a bird of repulsive habits, although as a devourer of every kind of garbage it may render some beneficial effects in the absence of sanitation.''

The second condition that interfered with our seeing tigers was the driving by our reserve guides, of whom we had three crammed into the front of a weird closed bush vehicle which could only have been made in India. Those of us who had avoided Delhi belly were sandwiched into the back seats that faced outwards and we proceeded into the sanctuary at a cracking pace, the driver slamming on brakes fiercely whenever anything presented itself, depositing most of us on the floor of the vehicle.

Occasional peacocks panicked at our arrival and sped off into the jungle, uttering the awful cries that only peacocks can muster. I'm not at my best when crowded into a tourist vehicle but walking was definitely prohibited and all afternoon we proceeded at hectic speed. Believe it or not, the next morning a few of us did catch a fleeting glimpse of a tiger which crossed the road hunting chital deer.

In 1922 the Maharajah of Alwan built a hunting lodge in what is now the Sariska Sanctuary. He is reputed to have shot more than two hundred tigers. In 1958 the lodge closed and the area was set aside for wildlife. By 1973 when Project Tiger was launched, there were only fourteen tigers left

there and their seemingly certain extinction was averted just in time by the wide-ranging measures taken as part of the project.

Operation Tiger was a campaign begun in India, Mrs. Ghandi setting an example that inspired the rest of Asia. India's segment of the campaign was called Project Tiger. With undertakings from the World Wildlife Fund to supply a million dollars' worth of equipment and scientific expertise – funded prominently by print sales of David Shepherd's painting "Tiger Fire" – the Indian government designated a series of tiger reserves, on which it has spent many times that sum. Because reserve planning affected entire ecosystems, the whole spectrum of other creatures and vegetation benefitted from the tiger conservation activity. In due course there were sixteen tiger sanctuaries, and by the time we visited, a decade of endeavour had strengthened the Bengal tiger's position from a total population of some 1 600 to about 3 000.

Sariska became a tiger sanctuary in 1978. It is an awe-inspiring reserve, hilly, with rocky rims clad in thick vegetation described as "tropical dry deciduous scrub jungle". It is one of the extreme limits of tiger distribution. Some 200 kilometres from Delhi, it covers an area of 210 square kilometres. Summers are extremely hot, with temperatures rising to forty-six degrees centigrade dur-

Tiger track

ing May and June. The monsoon between July and September brings most of the rain – an annual average of about 650 millimetres. Winters are severe with frost occurring in January. There are about thirty tigers in the sanctuary. We saw chital, a beautiful spotted deer which has declined drastically throughout India; sambar, the largest deer in Asia and, like the chital, preyed upon by tigers; and we saw langur, jackal, porcupine, jungle cat, mongoose, palm civet, hares, caracal and honey badger. Forest hog, leopard, nilgai and wild dog also occur. The birdlife is prolific, the most conspicuous birds being grey partridge, bush quail and peafowl.

Since the area is not fenced, there is human pressure on the boundaries, and there are also problems with water holes drying out. Large herds of cattle enter the sanctuary, creating pressure on grazing and water. Sariska thus has its fair share of troubles, but there is no arguing with the fact that the tiger population has increased dramatically.

From India we headed north for Katmandu, gateway to the Himalayas and the jungles of Chitwan, Nepal's most famous national park. Based at Tiger Tops lodge we saw Asian rhinos and at last got good views of the legendary tiger, of which some forty-five live in Chitwan. The position at Tiger tops was very different from that at Sariska.

greater one-horned rhino .

Here was a commercial operation which bent over backwards to help tourists – at a price. Staff worked hard at showing visitors their wildlife and Anton and I took advantage of all the opportunities provided to see tiger: from elephant back, from a baited blind and, by special arrangement, on foot. We saw a magnificent tiger at a buffalo calf bait.

But it was not quite the same as the experiences we later had while doing some jungle trekking on foot with Dan Bahada, an expert tiger tracker. With Dan we came across a large rhino bull in a densely wooded stream course, feeding on bamboo. Completely undetected, we were able to observe him for nearly thirty minutes. He was very noisy going about his feeding and we were therefore able to get up fairly close. Apart from tigers, which may take their young, these rhinos fear nothing except perhaps people. They were once widely distributed over the flood plains of the Indian subcontinent. Fewer than 1500 now remain, of which 400 live in Chitwan; most of the rest are in Kaziranga National Park in Assam, India. Compare this with the two African species, with about 7500 collectively 4000 remaining in the wild. Hunted and harassed for decades, these living relics of a bygone age survive today under very strict protection. Demand for rhino horn is a real danger to all rhino populations, but a greater threat is posed in Asia by a simple lack of space.

Attaining a height of over 183 centimetres and a mass of over two tons, the huge one-horned rhino with its unique armour-plated looking folded skin presents a strangely prehistoric appearance. Yet with a little more space it may still be brought back from its dangerously low numbers. In Chitwan, the situation warrants optimism. The rhinos have reached the stage where their population is now greater than the park can comfortably sustain and they wander beyond park boundaries where they come into contact with the farming community. According to K. K. Gurung, they sometimes become a positive menace. Successes with rhino in Chitwan are attributable to the excellent conservation work carried out by the Nepalese authorities since establishment of the park in 1973. However, as with similar situations in southern Africa and elsewhere, parks can become overcrowded by certain species and it becomes necessary to cull or translocate animals. Land acquisition for parks is invariably very difficult owing to the needs of the ever-expanding human population.

The most immediate danger for the one-horned rhino lies in the fact that the areas in which they are located are really very small. In Chitwan a mysterious disease afflicting the rhino underscored the problem of conserving them in limited areas. For this reason, the Asian Rhino Specialist Group of the International Union for the

carrying firewood.

Conservation of Nature and Natural Resources (IUCN) has worked to identify suitable alternative conservation areas that can accommodate rhino as well.

While out for three days with Dan Bahada, we found fresh tiger tracks in the mud alongside the clear stream where our camp was situated. With four porters we walked through the jungle in search of animal life, marvelling all the while at this beautiful 580-square-kilometre wilderness sandwiched between the Himalayas and a swelling sea of humanity. As is the case in many tiger areas in India, in Nepal's Chitwan valley former rulers had organised large tiger hunts. Trained elephants carrying invited viceroys of India and royalty of Europe ringed tiger and rhino and bagged large numbers of these animals.

With a clear view of the snow-capped Himalayas I was reminded of the words of George Schaller in his book *Mountain Monarchs*: "For epochs to come the peaks will still pierce the lonely vistas, but when the last snow leopard has stalked the crags and the last markhor has stood on a promontory, his ruff waving in the breeze, a spark of life will have gone, turning the mountains into stones of silence."

Schaller's words ring true for the one-horned Asian rhino and the tiger too. Should they vanish from their jungle home, something for me will forever be lost, even though the distance separating us is great. At night on the trail I lay in my tiny tent knowing that the tiger was out there somewhere and the thrill of being in tiger country kept me awake for most of the night. They are a crucial part of the living fabric of that magical land.

9.
Ivory and Elephant Men

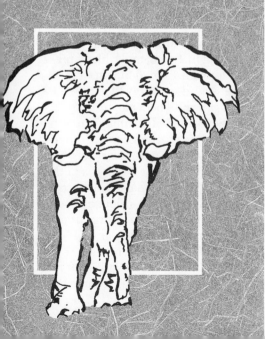

We walked silently among the skulls and jawbones of hundreds of rhino and elephant. What stunning waste — what miserable relics. We can fly to the moon, give people new hearts, decode DNA to manipulate the genetics of plants for agricultural miracles, but we can't seem to keep the leviathans of the wildlife world alive.

We were on an outing to Tsavo East in Kenya. A few of us stopped at a famous viewing spot known as Mudando Rock where I had taken a picture in 1961. Almost twenty years later the same location looked like a blasted minefield. Thousands of elephants had crammed into the park, forced into Tsavo by agriculture and the depredations of poachers. Drought and the decision not to cull elephants meant the animals stripped the park vegetation, changing the entire landscape. And then, with nothing more to eat, they died in their thousands. Such rhino as poachers didn't get died from lack of food. The Tsavo story is not mine; it belongs to people like David Sheldrick, and Peter Beard, who portrayed the senselessness of it all in his book, *The End of the Game*.

It was April, 1980. I had attended an International Union for the Conservation of Nature and Natural Resources (IUCN) conference on rhino and elephant in Nairobi, followed by a Rhino and Elephant Specialist Group meeting in Tsavo National Park.

Any South African was at that stage *persona non grata* in most African countries, but through the offices of the Department of Foreign Affairs and with considerable help from Charles Enjongo, Kenya's then attorney general, the way had been paved for a number of South African specialists to attend.

Dr. Anthony Hall-Martin, then a senior research officer with the South African National Parks Board, was among them. He had offered the Endangered Wildlife Trust his services as a scientific advisor, and a kinship had sprung up as so often does between those who share a concern for particular species. A third person was to come into my sphere of interest at the conference, although it was a few years later before Peter Hitchins, a specialist in black rhino, and I got to know one another well.

Anthony and I spent many hours between sessions driving around Tsavo in Dr. Iain Douglas-Hamilton's Land Cruiser. I never once caught even a glimpse of a rhino, but Anthony was luckier. With the aid of a Super Cub piloted by Tsavo warden Bill Woodley he spotted a few. Iain, author of *Among the Elephants*, had announced back in 1977 at the World Wilderness Congress in Johannesburg the estimate of 1 300 000 elephants left in Africa. I had corresponded with him for some time and prior to the congress I had

arranged through EWT a flying trip to Tuli for Iain and his wife Oria. We spent three delightful days looking at the Tuli elephants as guests of Monty Fuhr who owned Tuli Lodge on the banks of the Limpopo.

Iain had invited me then to join the Rhino and Elephant Specialist Group as a consultant. He encouraged me to turn my attention to elephant conservation, and this led me toward deepening concern about the ivory trade. I was later to disagree with Iain on his attitude towards ivory, but I always respected his efforts in drawing attention to the species more than anyone I know.

Sir Peter Scott was our chairman during the specialist group meeting in Tsavo, and a bleak picture was painted for rhino and elephant in most parts of Africa. Little did we know then how much bleaker things would become: in 1980 black rhino in Africa were still estimated to number 15 000, while by this writing they are down around 3 000. Uganda was a particularly sad example at the time. Iain and Eric Edroma of the Uganda Institute of Ecology revealed the horrifying extent to which that country's elephant population had collapsed. Much of the destruction had been caused by automatic rifles, and Ugandans weren't the only ones to blame. Tanzania's armed forces played a significant role. I think it was here in Tsavo that we all came to realise that saving all of Africa's elephants and rhinos was a lost cause, and although the South Africans and Zimbabweans present drew some comfort from the knowledge of sound elephant management in our countries, the overall picture was depressing.

Ian Parker of Nairobi played the devil's advocate. He repeatedly brought us back to earth by highlighting the pointlessness of pouring money into hopeless situations. One soon realised that the IUCN had put tens of thousands of dollars into projects where it certainly did not look as if the money had been wisely spent. We from South Africa were exempt from such criticism, because in most instances we had been overlooked for funding as the western world has a strong tendency to think that South Africa has all the money she needs.

I presented a paper on the South African ivory trade, which I believed was in need of investigation. Much of the ivory ascribed to South Africa, mainly in Hong Kong official trade statistics, was not South African in origin, but was shipped via South Africa to the Far East. Zimbabwean visitors, for example, brought carved ivory across the border and flooded the local market, in order to obtain currency outside their own country, which had very strict controls concerning foreign exchange.

I was against the ivory trade and drew much press attention to our local position. I had a lot to learn and while I shared many points of view with my friends the Douglas-Hamiltons, I was coming under the influence of Anthony Hall-Martin and the National Parks Board approach to the ivory question. In addition I was much influenced by an ivory trader I knew – the same John Ilsley who had been a police officer in Bechuanaland in my ranger days in the late 1960s.

With the co-operation of Graham Ferreira of the Argus Group, we set about drawing attention to quirks of the ivory trade in southern Africa. By comparison with the rest of Africa, the volume of ivory moving through South Africa was very small. However, the question of statistics bothered me. Official reports never tallied with the Hong Kong figures, and furthermore the trade figures issued by the government department concerned could not be reconciled with the customs statistics. When these were compared with Hong Kong figures, the situation was even more confusing. In fact South Africa had no idea how much ivory was leaving the country, and to make matters worse, the customs union with our neighbouring countries allowed ivory to enter South Africa without scrutiny.

Ivory originating in Zambia would enter Botswana and then be shipped out via South

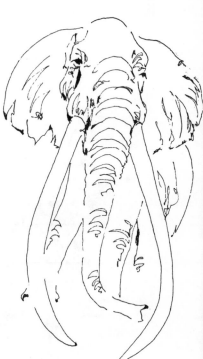

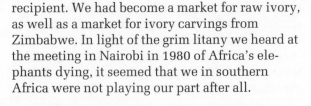

Africa, and upon arrival in Hong Kong it would be ascribed to South Africa in official statistics. We in South Africa looked as though we were producing a fairly large amount of ivory. Who, we asked, was killing so many elephants? The official supplies of ivory came only from our national parks and their output was known to be much less than that ascribed to South Africa by Hong Kong.

Dr. Jonas Savimbi of the rebel movement UNITA in Angola repeatedly claimed that he traded ivory in exchange for essential supplies such a medicine, and he named South Africa as the recipient. We had become a market for raw ivory, as well as a market for ivory carvings from Zimbabwe. In light of the grim litany we heard at the meeting in Nairobi in 1980 of Africa's elephants dying, it seemed that we in southern Africa were not playing our part after all.

Smuggling certainly occurred and few if any controls were in force. As to how many elephants were dying, no one knew. Our national parks were being criticised for elephant culling; they were sensitive on the ivory issue and had nothing but contempt for conservationists who opposed the trade. I decided to look into the position more closely and stay out of the press. If I could assess things unemotionally, I might be able to develop a more useful approach. I turned to my ivory trader friend for advice and soon began to realise that legitimate traders did not wish to see Africa's elephants disappear. A continual decline in elephant numbers would mean that they themselves would suffer.

On the other hand, much of the rest of Africa did not share that view. Elephants continued and continue to decline in their thousands. The conservation lobby, opposing the trade, is perhaps almost as much to blame for the demise of elephants as the illegal dealers who encourage peasants out in the bush to risk their lives killing elephants. The anti-ivory trade movement has so capitalised on emotional concerns that it has lost sight of the other real threat to elephants: human expansion into the domain of the elephant. Now that the trade has been outlawed by the Convention of International Trade in Endangered Species of Fauna and Flora (CITES) – although there are provisons for countries to apply for exemption – who will pursue the matter of ensuring that the remaining elephants have safe havens to live in? How will the effort be funded?

Don't let me give the impression that trade in ivory is not a threat. It certainly is. But one needs a balanced approach to the question, and I'm not sure we've arrived at one yet.

On the traii in the Tuli Block we once tracked a group of elephant along the banks of the Limpopo River which, apart from a few deep pools at its confluence with the Shashe River, was dry. About twelve elephants had come down the steep banks which countless heavy feet had worn away to create a funnel through which they moved to and fro. We had stationed ourselves on a small island and lay in the warm sun watching their movements.

In the distance we heard the clinking of cow bells and sure enough, some twenty cows came around the bend ahead of us and soon moved up among the elephant. I recall remarking how odd the

scene was. On the Botswana side of the river was a place of refuge for elephants, and on the Transvaal bank the elephant very definitely were not welcome. Intensive land use practices have completely put paid to any hope of expanding the Tuli elephant range, either in Botswana or in South Africa. Electrical fences and occasionally guns keep the elephants at bay. It's a case of diminishing range and an expanding elephant population.

Here, as elsewhere, the elephants have nowhere to go and so they bounce back and forth, harassed by people in one way or the other. To be perfectly sensible, considering the circumstances, it would be best to reduce the number of elephant, use the meat locally, make the ivory and hides available to the trade, and prevent the kind of habitat destruction that occurred in Tsavo. But now trade in elephant products is illegal, and anyway there has been resistance down through the years to culling in the Tuli.

It takes courage, in this debate, to fire the first shot. Few wish to do it.

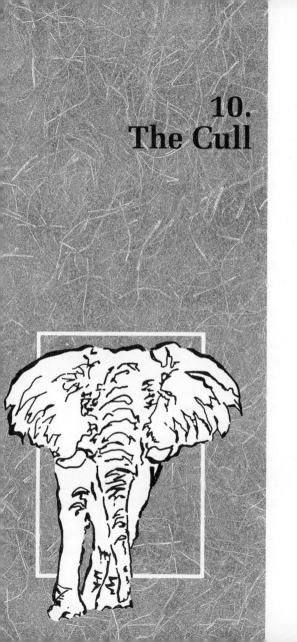

10.
The Cull

Culling of elephants as we know it in southern Africa is the systematic destruction of entire family units and this practice has been carried out in the Kruger National Park and the parks of Zimbabwe for some years.

In order to understand more fully the ivory story, I wrote to Dr. David Cummings of the research staff of Zimbabwe's wildlife agency, with whom I had become acquainted as a result of the Rhino and Elephant Specialist Group meeting in Kenya in 1980. I wanted a firsthand account of how Zimbabwe managed elephant populations and he promptly wrote back arranging for me to visit a cull in Wankie National Park, now known as Hwange. I had been up in Botswana leading a trail in the Okavango and arranged for my colleague and fellow EWT trustee Peter Joffe to fly up and meet me in Maun, from where we headed east across the dry thornveld of Botswana toward Victoria Falls. We were flying in Peter's Mooney four-seater single-engine aircraft. Below us the bushveld rolled right up to the border. It was my first visit since the country had become Zimbabwe, and very well received we were.

After refuelling we passed the falls and headed south for Hwange National Park. Unbeknown to us, there are two airstrips, one in the park and one just outside built to cater for Wankie Safari Lodge.

We landed on this vast runway and taxied up to the deserted terminal building. After sitting around for half an hour we realised no one was coming to meet us, and figured there had to be another strip. We weren't airborne long before we found the park strip and touched down as a dark green Land Rover drove up with park biologist Drew Conneybere behind the wheel. A research officer studying elephants, Drew was to take charge of us for the next few days and would accompany us into the field. We loaded our gear and headed down to meet his wife and collect his equipment. We were to camp out in the north-east near Intunye Dam together with the culling team. A two-hour journey took us to our camp alongside a dry river. It was the month of July and we had brought along sleeping bags, being under the impression that we would be accommodated in tents.

This was not to be, however. We found ourselves sleeping out on a canvas sail near the kitchen set up by the rangers' wives. The culls go on for weeks at a time and some of the staff bring along their wives to look after them. Peter and I soon sampled a stew made from the pounded flesh of elephant. This was to be expected as there was certainly a good deal of fresh meat handy; somewhat to my surprise, fresh elephant meat turned out to be in a culinary class of its own.

The river bed where camp was set up was no different from most river beds – it got extremely cold at night. Water froze in a twenty-litre container left uncovered. What a long night. Dawn was a welcome relief as we stiffly struggled out of our bags and gratefully accepted coffee. Soon a Piper Super Cub roared over our heads piloted by Rick Clough and all we had to do was sit back and wait while he sought out a manageable-sized group of elephant. The rest of the camp was active as radios, weapons, vehicles and equipment were made ready.

We did not have long to wait before the pilot radioed that a group of twenty-eight animals had been located. Drew, Peter and I were assigned to Clem Coetzee's vehicle which charged out of camp followed by an assortment of other vehicles loaded with gear and twenty-five people. After half an hour we picked up the circling Cub.

Coetzee was in radio communication with the pilot and soon gave out quiet orders. Everyone knew their job and they went calmly about their tasks. Peter and I were instructed to stay close behind Clem and Torre Ballance who, together with Terry Roche, would make up the gunmen. All were kitted out like spacewalkers with backpack radios and bright orange flashes to make them highly visible to each other. Armed with heavy calibre rifles, they were in turn backed up by three assistants carrying automatic weapons. Others carried lengths of stout rope to be used in tying up suitable-sized baby elephants selected for capture, later to be sold to zoos and safari parks.

The operation in Zimbabwe takes the following pattern. Parks staff, often rangers drawn from reserves around the country, cull whole family units of elephants. The government retains the ivory and private contractors tender for the hide and meat, bringing in their own teams and equipment. A bush abattoir is set up where the meat and hides are cleaned. The meat is cut up in a special cutting machine and laid out on long flat wire beds about a metre wide. The hides after cleaning are salted and stacked before being shipped out to the main centres.

The pilot radioed to Clem that the herd was moving away from us in light open mopane woodland about two kilometres away and told us to get a move on in order to cut them off. The herd, which had numbered twenty-eight when first sighted, had split up and this group now numbered seventeen, a comfortable number to handle. We set off on the run and I quickly felt somewhat winded. I realised I was not as fit as these men. Soon the lead elephant came into view moving at a fair pace. The scene before us was one of unreality. The herd had no idea of our

Kudu bull
'92

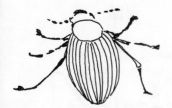

presence and rolled on through the bush toward us. The three men whose job it was to shoot the oncoming elephant moved ahead of us and took up their positions. I stuck close behind Clem as he ran forward, and the group matriarch came steadily toward us, only to be felled in seconds. Other elephants started to mill around and then also fell to the fusillade of shots.

I recall looking over the bodies of fallen elephants and seeing Peter with one of the gunmen on the opposite side from where I was. I remember no trumpeting or screaming except by the young elephants being chased by some of the team as other men leaped onto their backs to slow them down. One youngster stood tied to its dead mother and another resisted all attempts to pull him down and went off dragging three men. Peter later recalled seeing where bullets had exited from the heads of animals that had been shot from our side. Both he and Terry Roche were at some risk; later I heard that a culling team member was accidentally shot on a cull in Gonarezhou.

All thirteen adult elephant were down in thirty-five seconds and three small ones were captured. The fourth youngster was shot after all as it was a male, and only females were wanted by the buyers. It was all over. Everyone now sat down under some trees to await the tractor, which could be heard approaching, bringing the teams who would do the skinning and butchering.

The task for Clem and his team was over for the day, having taken a total of less than three hours from take-off by the Super Cub to firing the last shot. My own recollections are slightly unclear as everything happened so quickly. Culling teams in Zimbabwe are efficient and their work is a no-nonsense affair. They are most certainly at risk and it's pretty tough work by comparison with the methods in the Kruger National Park, where the risk factor is much lower.

There had been no bravado in what we saw. I was interested to know whether these people enjoyed what they were doing and asked Drew what he thought. His reply was that he felt anyone who did a job well must enjoy it. I've heard tell that no one likes the work, and yet there is clearly an element of powerful excitement in it.

Probably the worst part of the operation is shortly after the adult cows are shot. The herd, in sheer panic, mills around the leader and other fallen members of the family, pushing, shoving, some even trying to climb up onto the lifeless forms as the culling team moves among them at close range to despatch them. At this stage the shooters use automatic weapons, which by now they have taken from their assistants, handing over the empty heavy calibre rifles used for the early, longer range shots.

Many conservationists and preservationists feel very strongly about the relative merits of culling elephants and letting nature take its course. If elephant numbers are allowed to increase too far, long term damage can be inflicted upon the habitat. Yet there is evidence that periodic habitat alteration of this kind has a place in the natural scheme of things . . . Ecologists in Zimbabwe and the Kruger National Park responsible for determining the off-take are adamant that the decisions are based on ecological grounds – aimed at retaining stability of habitat for all park wildlife – and not financial considerations, and I concur fully with those claims.

The exact numbers may nevertheless be questioned and I have met field men who are convinced that the numbers are often excessive. Differences of opinion between field men and researchers are not new in wildlife management, however. But one aspect that I believe is overlooked is social stress factors caused by culling. The prevailing idea is that by wiping out entire family units, the deed is wiped out with them. But this does not always seem to be the case.

I discussed this with Dr. Anthony Hall-Martin on a visit to the Kruger National Park and he agreed

that not enough was really known. "Family units" are culled, but each group is part of – and related to – a larger group. I had on a previous visit flown in the Parks Board helicopter on a culling operation in the northern sector of the park, and one incident stuck in my mind. We had picked up a large group of elephant near the Tsende River. From 1 200 feet we had an excellent view as the elephant started moving directly in front of us. I take up my field notes from that day, March 24, 1981:

The pilot is Hugo van Niekerk, flying helicopter ZS-HFO, time 3.10 – Elephant have broken up into small groups with the bulls running ahead. Directly below us we observe an enormous tusker and Anthony clearly is excited as it turns out no one has seen this bull elephant before. In my own excitement my camera jams and I have to be content with gazing down on this magnificent sight. (Little did I realize that this was the elephant that later was to be named João, one of the Kruger National Park's "magnificent seven" elephants of whom Mafunyane was the most famous. João later broke off both his tusks, Anthony believes in a battle with another bull in 1984. His ivory was estimated to weigh about seventy kilograms a side, the left being about 271 centimetres long and the right one about 250.) After protesting at our presence, for we have been hovering and turning directly above him for two or three min-

utes, Anthony's motor drive whirring away all the while, the bull crashes through some dense bush and, holding his head aloft, defiantly glares at the helicopter as we turn away.

3.20 – Herd now running, now standing. Hugo moves the chopper forward and the herd starts to run again. Altitude 400 feet. Occasional big elephant turn and face the helicopter. Now tightly bunched and standing. Big bull breaks to the right and takes off and Hugo passes sharply over the herd, swings to the right and holds his position.

3.25 – Elephant move off and we break right and climb to 1500 feet. All Hugo's skills and years of flying on elephant culls come into play. The elephant are now resting in a mopane thicket as Hugo wipes his hands a few times on his leg. Apart from an occasional word on the radio to Kobus Botha, the ranger sitting behind him, Hugo is now fully concentrating on manoeuvering this group toward a firebreak road where the ground crew is waiting.

3.30 – Elephant move off and I notice two slip in the mud. They are very conscious of the sound of the Bell Jet Ranger and the thudding of its rotors I'm sure sets up a similar quickening beat within each elephant's chest. I notice two young bulls on the left flank making a total of twenty-seven which is far too many for the ground crew to handle. Impala stand confused as elephant run past them and a warthog family races off ahead of the moving group.

culling elephant

3.33 – The large bull we watched break from the herd earlier rejoins them. Cows occasionally place their trunks across the backs of their babies and are clearly agitated. The big bull runs off to one side and faces the helicopter. One wonders what is going on in his mind. As he turns and departs we don't pursue him as he is not our objective.

3.35 – Elephant now race off in single file, emptying their bowels as they flee towards a dry river bed where they pause for a moment and then move off again, the cows throwing up water onto themselves and their young. We are thirty feet above them, hovering one second and then slowly pushing them forward the next.

We approach a tar road and Hugo races the helicopter forward to get them across quickly and away from being observed by tourists. We are now near a firebreak. He has positioned the ground team and we are so low that I can smell the elephant as we move directly over the single line of twelve running animals, the final number. Hugo, who directs the operation, announces we are going in as Kobus prepares himself in the open door of the helicopter and makes a final check on his immobilising gun loaded with the drug scoline. The time is 3.40.

3.45 – First a big cow and a sub-adult are darted.

3.46 – A further two.

3.47 – Two more attempt to move off and are darted.

3.48 – Two more and one cow is now down. The matriarch is still on her feet but all have slowed down and are lurching. One cow has fallen on top of her baby as we circle left and right, holding them together.

3.49 – Four are down; two already darted start tusking one another.

3.50 – The lead cow goes down on her brisket and then onto her side while two calves stand pressed against their fallen mothers. The big cow struggles to rise as the vehicles move in at 3.55 and Eric Wood races in with a rifle to despatch any that appear alive. All are down bar two babies, which are given shots of M99 as they are to be captured alive and later sold. Hugo lands the helicopter some distance away and I climb out to join the ground crew. I am not allowed to take any photographs. The Parks Board is rigid about this, fearing negative publicity.

As the trucks and large tractor move in, the throats of all the fallen elephant are cut and they are disemboweled. Anthony, meanwhile, is giving his assistant instructions on the sample mate-

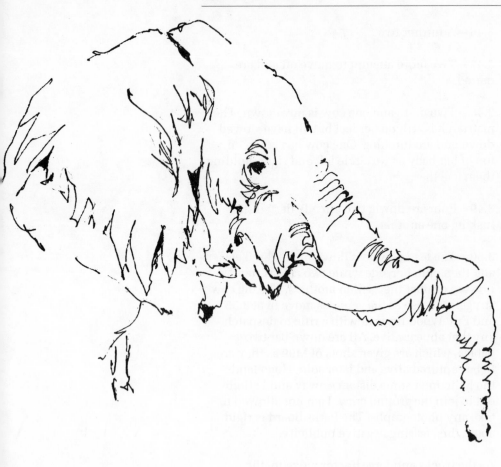

rial he requires. Someone announces that a bull elephant is approaching. We jump up onto the Land Cruiser and sure enough, the large bull that had been with the herd is now some three hundred metres away and cautiously approaching us through stunted mopane with trunk upraised. He shows no fear and is clearly interested.

It is quite clear to me that he is not being aggressive, although this view is not shared by Eric Wood who promptly hauls a rifle out of his vehicle and intends to use it. I am puzzled at his concern and ask Anthony why he appears alarmed. Anthony in turn asks Eric, who replies that he is responsible for the safety of staff and equipment and is taking no chances. The bull is by now fairly close and Eric places a shot over his head which causes him to move off. Although in no hurry and still curious, he retires into a thicket.

That bull elephant surely knew things were not right. What about the others in the original larger group of twenty-seven? How much did they know or see? What did they make of the damp earth where the bodies had fallen? Could they recognize smells in the gut piles, or did the vultures consume those before any elephants came close? I don't think we have all the answers.

While I was in Anthony Hall-Martin's office in

March 1985 his assistant wandered in and announced that the culling unit was to take a number of bull elephants in the south of the park that afternoon. Would I like to go? This was my first opportunity to witness the culling of bull elephants. The reason for the operation was that bulls were foraging across the southern park boundary into sugar cane fields and citrus groves. The park authorities have had considerable trouble with elephants breaking through the southern fence, despite electrification of the fence. Bulls are in any event taken as part of the park's reduction programme, so in this case the reasons were twofold.

Anthony and I headed south in the direction of Berg-en-Dal, the then newly completed camp near the Malelane gate. I had previously stayed there and spent pleasant hours in search of game, and thought now how ironic: here I was on my way back, this time to witness the killing of the same species I had the previous year sought to enjoy.

Berg-en-Dal is sadly positioned, in my opinion, with a direct view of a sugar mill of all things, and fields of cane beyond the park border – the very reason for the control of elephant. We arrived at the home of the district ranger, to be met by Eric Wood, once again in charge of ground operations with his trucks and equipment. We

had already seen the park's blue and white Bell Jet Ranger piloted by Piet Otto flying upriver in search of a bull group. The chopper soon swooped down to where we were waiting and advised us where the elephant has been spotted: seven bull in all, close to the tar road. One chopper door was swiftly removed by a large Shangaan dressed in white overalls and hard hat. The ranger now climbed into the back with the immobilising gun and the loaded scoline darts, and with a roar the helicopter lifted off. We all bundled into vehicles and set off in hot pursuit.

No time was wasted as the parks' well-oiled machine got into action. The pilot herded the bulls with swift turns, often coming below the top of the tree canopy. We could clearly see the ranger firing his dart gun while Piet kept the bulls bunched.

The elephants milled around. One was a good tusker. I was so enthralled with the helicopter that I did not notice a vehicle parked near us full of wide-eyed tourists. If they wanted action, they certainly got it and were soon joined by another group. I wonder what they felt or whether they understood. Leaving them staring after us, we plunged off the road into the bush after Eric. Piet had radioed that the animals were down.

The sharp report of a rifle meant the ranger was

taking no chances and was anxious to avoid any suffering. At least three scoline darts were fired into each bull and then they were finished off with a rifle bullet. Four of the elephant lay on top of each other and the fifth lay a metre away. Eric shot two of the bulls where they lay in case any life remained as the field force moved in with highbed trailers, tractor, two-tonne trucks and a six-tonner with crane.

Throats were cut and stomachs opened by a small band of highly efficient men. Anthony's assistant collected samples and tags were affixed to each tongue for later identification of each skull. Within twenty minutes the work was done and the carcasses were being loaded onto the trucks which then headed for the abattoir at Skukuza. I wondered whether the surviving bulls had learned any lessons and what associations their fears had aroused and how they would react the next time a large, noisy blue and white bird appeared in the sky.

Whichever school of thought one may subscribe to as regards culling, and no matter how distasteful the killing is, we have created the situation and have no choice but to see it through honestly and with the best motives we can apply.

One incident in my experience of culling elephants which I shall not forget took place on the

Zimbabwean cull, and left me wondering what
it is about humans that sets us apart from the
beasts. After the rifles fell silent and the culling
team sat down to rest the ground team arrived
and took over the grisly job of cutting up the carcasses. I was wandering among them impressed
at the speed with which each group worked,
when Peter Joffe came over, led me to the back of
a Land Rover, and picked up one of two elephant
penises lying on the floor. The head of the
butchering operation had cut them off two young
bulls, and told Peter very matter-of-factly that he
would later have them skinned, cured and
mounted as lampstands for friends.

Dear Elephant, Sir, the beasts of the field fall in
more ways than one.

11.
Okavango

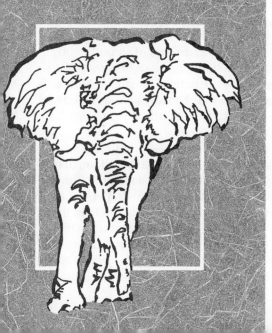

We set out after dinner with P. J., a spotlight and some trident spears. The idea was that with the aid of the spotlight we would spear some bream to feed to the fish eagles near Xaxaba the following day, and to provide the camp table with some excellent fish.

We all had a turn. In my enthusiasm when my turn came I plunged my spear down as hard as I could at a passing fish, and the force carried me clean out of the boat into the dark water of the Boro channel. I recall seeing the southern sky in all its majestic finery as I surfaced, and then realizing that the Boro had its fair share of crocodiles. P. J. yelled to me to stay calm and tread water as he spun the boat around and headed for me at top speed. As it came alongside I was quickly hauled on board, still clutching P. J.'s trident – minus, I might add, the fish.

That incident cemented the relationship that was established that night. Anyone who was crazy enough to fling himself overboard on a dark night into the Boro was alright in P. J.'s book. The old legend of "he who puts his pole in too deep stays with it" launched a lasting friendship for us. We were ready to begin our trailing venture into the Okavango.

For years I had dreamed of getting to the Okavango, the vast inland delta in the northern part of Botswana, thousands of islands yearly surrounded by an annual flood which finally dies in the Makgadikgadi pans. My chance came at last in 1978 with my Educational Wildlife Expeditions co-director Val Ford; Pirot Peroz, the pilot from our helicopter flying days of surveying the Tuli elephants; Mandy Mitchell from our office staff; and two friends. We headed north in a 210 Cessna Centurion six-seater single-engine aircraft, to research the possibility of establishing Okavango trails.

Our hosts were to be P.J. and Joyce Besterlink, Joyce being one of the daughters of the late Bobby Wilmot, pioneer of the Okavango. Crocodile hunter, transport rider, explorer, he had been one of the first to establish a camp near Maun. Although originally built for his crocodile hunt-

ing operations, it later became a home for wildlife-viewing travellers. Joyce and P.J. had built a camp on the west side of the Boro channel when the original Xaxaba – built by Bobby's son Lloyd – closed down in the 1970s because the boundary of the Moremi Game Reserve was moved west to include Chief's Island with the Boro as its western border.

We arrived at lunch time and were not disappointed. The delta is the most enchanting place, guaranteed to enthrall anyone – let alone an artist. I instantly fell in love. We spent the afternoon in dugouts – the Bayei word for these wonderful vessels used to get around the delta's highways and byways is *mokoro*, plural *mekoro*. The Okavango Delta covers an area of some 15 000 square kilometres in the north of Botswana. One of the wonders of the natural world, breathtaking in its sheer vastness and beauty, a treasure chest of natural diversity and abundant in species . . . but fragile.

Three major ecotypes make up the system, distinguished by abundance or lack of water. In the far north is the permanent swamp, with perennial water up to four metres deep. This is where the Okavango River twists and turns down the panhandle of the delta. Crocodiles are numerous and dense stands of papyrus (*Cyperus papyrus*) are the home to the shy and seldom-seen sitatunga,

(*Tragelaphus spekei*) known by the local Bayei as *nakong*.

The second ecotype consists of seasonally-inundated areas and hundreds of small islands covered in dense riparian woodland along the edges of the channels that get flooded. Here one finds an array of the beautiful trees that are such a feature of the Okavango. The *mukutshumo* or jackal berry (*Diospyros mespiliformis*) and sausage trees (*Kigela africana*) are notable for the fashioning of mekoro; the *matsaudi* or lowveld mangosteen (*Garcinia livingstonei*), was first described by Dr. Livingstone when he journeyed to the north-east of the delta. Some thirty-four species of large trees are found on these islands.

Finally, there are the dry land masses, which are slightly higher in altitude. Moremi Game Reserve, Chief's Island and the dry western sandveld make up this third major ecotype. Elephant, lion, buffalo, giraffe, red lechwe and baboons are but a few of the many mammals among the great diversity of species occurring here. There are numerous varieties of reptiles, some eighty species of fish and more than four hundred species of birds. The birdlife of the delta is one of its special delights. The first afternoon we were treated to everything from tiny kingfishers to fish eagles, squacco herons, slaty egrets and pygmy geese.

Around 1750 the Okavango saw the arrival of the Bayei, the first Bantu-speaking people to migrate to these parts from west of the confluence of the Chobe and Zambezi rivers. Punting, paddling and walking, they made their way into the Okavango Delta and settled alongside the channels and on islands, taking up a lifestyle of hunting and fishing similar to that they had practised at their former home. Their settlement was gradual and over the years they established such villages as Seronga, Sepopa, Gumare and Nokaneng, well-known place names in present-day Botswana. Today they are still the most numerous people in and about the delta, numbering some 16 000. Their traditional pursuits enable them to live harmoniously within this environment.

For us, leaving the smoky environment of Pretoria and Johannesburg and finding ourselves a few hours later transported into this new world, the effect was electrifying. I can put it no other way. The same year we ran six five-day trails into the delta. In the years to come this built up to thirty each year, and we have thus given this same pleasure of discovery to thousands of Okavango visitors.

My first trail was nearly my last, mind you. I was by no means well versed in the ways of travel in these distant parts. I brought all my hard-gained bush knowledge to bear, but I'm afraid I paid too

Flowers of the sausage tree

Saddlebill

little attention to the human factor, which nearly proved my undoing.

On our second day we arrived at an open stretch of water where there were numerous spurwing geese. In the centre was a small island with a large *mumu* fig tree (water fig, *Ficus verruculosa*), under which we planned to camp for the night. One of the Bayei mokoro polers, armed with an ancient rifle I noticed in his dugout, found the temptation irresistible. Before I realised what he was up to, we heard a loud report followed by frantic wingbeats as the geese, locally known as *sahuti*, struggled into the air in panic, leaving one of their own behind.

This was hurriedly retrieved by the proud hunter and no amount of complaining on my part made any difference. I made a silent note to tell P.J. that that poler was never coming along again, and furthermore, what was he doing shooting in a game reserve? We unpacked the dugouts and I set up camp while the luckless spurwing was systematically dismembered and cast into an iron pot. Lesson number one – people live here and they must eat, even if inside a game reserve.

I had invited a woman journalist from a leading magazine to accompany us, and also invited our pilot to spend four days gliding through the Okavango. I assigned them to the same mokoro

and the pilot and journalist were soon chatting happily as we set off into the wide blue yonder. We only had seven sleeping bags, but this presented no problem for the two newfound friends, who were quite happy to share everything.

The second lesson was at the expense of the journalist when she decided to take a swim in the cool clear channel that flowed by close to camp. She removed all her clothes and proceeded to dive into the water from a standing position in the dugout. The resulting splash and movement all but capsized the pilot in the dugout, and the journalist sped up the channel like Esther Williams. The effect on the other trailists was interesting to say the least, but they had not seen the last of the afternoon's excitement.

Our swimmer duly arrived back at the dugout and hauled herself in: a procedure which, when one is completely unclothed, is not the most glamorous way of climbing back on board. It did not take her long to discover that she had a very long, black, nasty leech firmly attached to her left breast. She threw her hands up in the air and yelled for help – not from me, for which I was grateful, but from our pilot. She was horrified and clearly did not know what to do. One way of removing leeches is to burn them with a cigarette end, but this seemed out of the question, and the pilot spent the next frantic few moments attempting to pull the leech off. When he succeeded, blood flowed down over the anguished woman's naked form.

We eventually restored some dignity to the scene and as our journalist covered herself up again, I acknowledged lesson number two: be careful about who you pair off in a dugout.

For the next few years we virtually had the western side of Chief's Island to ourselves and our trails grew in popularity. We learned a good deal from a Bayei elder named Mokabela, who worked for P.J., having set up his clan on a small island nearby. He was an expert in the ways of the Okavango and his interest in passing his knowledge on to others made a whole new world unfold.

One of the things Mokabela has taught me something about is lions. Lions are unpredictable. I have come to understand elephants in many ways, but I have never felt comfortable on foot, face to face with a lion. A three-day paddle by mokoro up the Boro from Xaxaba is Piajo, an inlet at one end of Chief's Island. Slowly paddling along these waterways, one is conscious of the presence of lion, although for the most part one hears rather than sees them. The Bayei treat them with both respect and contempt: contempt during the day, respect at night.

On one trail to this area, we had pitched camp on a beautiful point with a deep channel flowing by – a sheer delight after a long, hot day in the dugouts. I had named the place Moklawane, after a grove of beautiful ilala palms (*Hyphaene bengullensis*); Mokabela had told me the Tswana name for these graceful palms. As the sun dipped down towards the western plains of the Okavango, the early evening came alive with the sounds of frogs and insects. It was a magical world, with a deep mauve treeline and azure-blue sky, great white egrets in flight appearing motionless against this vast backdrop. We heard the plaintive shrill cry of unseen pygmy geese. Our fire blazed against the darkening sky as we discussed the day's happenings. For most in my party of eight, this was their first venture into the delta and they were understandably overawed by it.

Mokabela and his team chattered away as they prepared their dinner of mealie meal and fish, previously smoke-dried and boiled. We discussed them while they discussed us, carefully weighing up each new trail member. Six Bayei were in our group, one the baggage master, and the rest polers. Amidst their laughter, throat clearing, and spitting came the low far-off call of a lion. The Bayei picked it up quickly and hushed our idle chatter. We all listened and peered into the darkness.

Fisheagle

Finally, with nervous laughter, someone placed more wood on the fire and I tried to convince trailists that they had nothing to fear. I wondered if they believed me, for experience had taught me that the lions of the Okavango will cross large areas of water, swimming where necessary, as they follow the buffalo herds. The whole area is inundated from May to September and the buffalo are continually on the move, with the lions not far behind. By nine most of us were under mosquito nets, huddled together near the fire. A lion grunt from across the channel was answered by another, some distance away. They were on

the move now as we settled down, gazing up through the mosquito netting at the star-studded sky. I knew that lions had sometimes taken sleeping people who had not taken precautions, but it did not seem likely that night as we drifted off to sleep.

At four in the morning I was sitting at the low fire thinking, when a series of lion grunts woke Mokabela and he rose and came over, as usual the first up among the Bayei. It was mid-July and a cold wind wafted over the water, sending a shiver up my back. Before long a scrub robin began calling in the undergrowth, followed shortly by noisy red-billed francolin. Dawn was upon the Okavango; time to stir sleeping forms with coffee and rusks.

Gliding across the dead flat water among upthrusting grass stems encrusted with countless tiny droplets of dew, Mokabela led us to where the lions had been when last heard. The mokoros' wooden snouts pushed through ever tighter grass and reeds until we beached silently and prepared to start walking in the cool of early morning.

Three Bayei led and the rest followed in the rear as we set off in single file. I had told my group to walk as quietly as possible and what to do should we encounter lion: first and foremost never to run, under any circumstances. Armed with an

Buffalo skull —
lion kill in the
okavango

assortment of cane knives, *selepes* (a type of axe), and my old .458, we made our way through a dense stand of knob-thorn and giraffe acacia. It was almost impossible to remain silent. Carpets of leaves and branches heralded our arrival as we passed from one stand of bush into an opening of soft sand and plunged into the next thicket. But there was no talking except when I stopped to explain some point of interest, or we paused for a cigarette break and drink of water. The sun was warm and the party began to feel the pace. Chief's Island is rockless and consists of soft Kalahari sand, hard on thighs and calves.

We swung away from a long-since dry pan area where baboon droppings and tracks of lion, buffalo, impala and tsessebe were evident in the fine powdery dust. Following a game trail, we crossed a grove of camel thorn trees that had seen the recent passing of elephant – we saw dry dung, stripped bark and broken branches with their long white thorns, easily capable of penetrating tennis shoes – but there was little fresh evidence of lion. Mokabela was still in the lead and Patrick followed, bearing my rifle. By ten, the sun was burning our foreheads, necks and backs.

We were moving across a grassy opening when Mokabela shouted, "Lion!" Both he and Patrick rushed forward. A big male raced across the clearing in front of us, followed by another male

and a lioness with two cubs. Not realizing that there were two *more* lionesses, but jolted into sudden shock by Mokabela's shout and the rapid action, we didn't anticipate the now furious charge of first one lioness and then the second. The effect was amazing – the trail party froze, but not Mokabela and team, who immediately started yelling and abusing the onrushing lioness. Sand and dust flew as she came to a halt five paces from our group, all of us rivetted to the spot and silent.

I recall seeing Patrick near me; he had made no attempt to use or hand me my rifle, but was haranguing the lioness. Her bluff called, she was lashing her sides with her tail, her companion standing behind her. They backed off, growling, retreated, and then one came at us a second time. By now, I had retrieved my rifle and was waiting for the worst, although the speed at which a lion charges would make it very difficult to fire.

No one in the group uttered a word. All were downright terrified. Then when the tension was released and the lions gone, no one could stop talking. I manoeuvred them to a large antheap, so as to take no risks in the tall grass, and there we remained for half an hour while everyone calmed down. It was interesting that they had behaved as instructed. The Bayei did not seem unduly alarmed. During the charge, I even contemplated pulling Patrick in front of me, as he was armed not only with my rifle but also with a selepe and seemed far less concerned than I was.

Their contempt – familiarity may be a better word – was illustrated again on another occasion in the same area, when we surprised a number of lions on a buffalo carcass. Almost instantly, the men began raising their voices. The lions started backing off and the polers advanced in a group towards the remaining two, one an adult lioness. Their choice of language was apparently too much for her: she reluctantly abandoned the kill, which turned out to be a full-grown bull. Five or six lions had been successfully driven off and I was to learn about something that has gone on in

the African bush for decades, finding lion kills and robbing the owners of the spoils. Our polers quickly set to work, cutting off the choicest pieces of flesh, and were soon laden down with meat.

Growth of tourism, inevitably, has been a mixed blessing. A camp starts off in a small way but grows as demand increases. More people are required to attend to the needs of tourists. More dugouts are needed, villages grow, fishing increases. Even the hippo suffer for as more dugouts take to the water, the hippo "menace" increases. More of the flood plain is burned for it is easier to pole a mokoro through shallow water unimpeded by the debris of last year's grass and reeds. More game is attracted to the burned areas, were fresh new growth of grass appears; poaching increases, and this includes elephant. The benefits to the Bayei are the chance to be employed, a steady income, and sales of baskets. Conservationists protest at the invasion of the Okavango. Safari operators have to make a profit, but they would not wish to destroy their own livelihood by promoting excessive tourist development.

Ten years ago only small groups of people populated islands west of the Boro. Today a huge settlement is to be found close to two tourist camps. The impact on a fragile system must be felt. There

is an upsurge in tourism to the Okavango and strict controls will have to be enforced in both tourism and utilization of the delta.

One very important control is the barrier known as the Buffalo Fence which presently extends from the east, south past Maun, then up the western sandveld side of the Okavango to a point east of the village of Gumare. This fence is intended to keep cattle from coming into contact with buffalo, because of the threat of foot-and-mouth disease. But it also keeps livestock out of the delta. Fly across the Buffalo Fence and it is all too plain what effect livestock has had on this fragile ecosystem. The delta could be ruined in very short order. Twice while taking pictures from the air I have seen cattle and goats moving along below as a huge ball of dust rose up to meet me. Outside the fence the rangeland is badly damaged, and there are problems of cattle moving around the fence at the north end. In the western panhandle of the Okavango it is not uncommon to see lechwe and cattle together. Once I saw a herd of thirty buffalo not far from cattle grazing up to their bellies in water.

In July 1983, I flew to Botswana with *National Geographic* senior writer Tom Canby, who was researching drought conditions throughout the world for a major story. We set out to assess the effects of the drought in Botswana, particularly

the Okavango and the Savuti area of Chobe National park. We had by then extended our Okavango trails to include two days at Savuti, to show trailists the big game for which that area is renowned. Up to 1982 the crystal clear waters of the Savuti channel all the way from the Linyanti swamp to the Savuti marsh had been a mecca for many species. But as our aircraft droned across the Kalahari's dry vastness in 1983, I told Tom what to expect at Savuti, for the previous year the channel had stopped flowing.

Maun, the gateway to the wildlife of northern Botswana, lay dry and dusty – very much as it always looked at that time of year. However, one thing was different. The Boteti River was nowhere near as high as was usual during July and further to the east, towards the

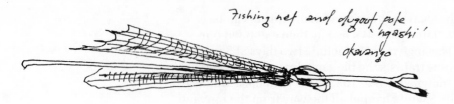

Fishing net and dugout pole 'ngashi' okavango

Makgadikgadi, it was bone dry. The Okavango had not brought down the volume of water experienced in previous years and much of the delta was low. Savuti to the north-east was not much better: the channel was dry all the way to the Linyanti swamp. Between Moremi and Savuti, in the dry mopane veld, we observed pans still holding rain water and it was here that we saw numerous herds of elephants. The thousands of buffalo often seen in the Savuti area were absent. So was the heavy concentration of elephant, which had moved north and west into the mopane woodlands. The fish had all died, the hippos and crocodiles had started to leave. The

Savuti channel, with its characteristic dead trees, was a mass of weeds and grass.

Drought is nothing unusual. It is a natural occurrence, one of the mechanisms checking wildlife populations. Most wildlife in the Okavango and Savuti was not unduly affected, although it's hard for conservationists not to feel wrenched by the dryness of the woodlands, or the sight of bull elephants waiting patiently to drink from three or four water seeps, or twenty-one hippos crammed in a mud hole.

But the game does disperse and this is one of the beauties of northern Botswana: it is vast, and wildlife still has room to move – unlike in South Africa where no such situation exists. It will take courage and bold decisions for Botswana to come to terms with her tourism potential, and the need to conserve wildlife resources to make the most of that potential.

And decisiveness is indeed coming to the fore. In recent years Botswana has embarked upon a series of actions that bode well for the future. A national tourism policy aimed at high-cost, low-volume tourism is gaining currency. Water development plans acknowledge the key importance of not interfering with the ecology of the core area of the Okavango Delta. Extension of the boundaries of Moremi Game Reserve is under discus-

sion. An elephant management plan is develop-
ing. The conservation authorities are on the move.
With stunning wild treasures like the Okavango
and the Central Kalahari to safeguard, Botswana
is well advised to devote considerable effort to
ensuring that her distinctive natural heritage is
not squandered.

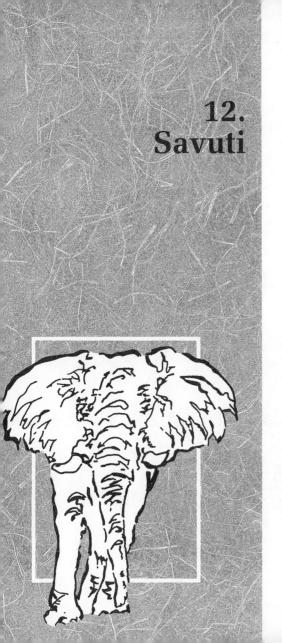

12.
Savuti

Elephants have not been plunging in numbers everywhere in Africa. One place where the destruction of large numbers of elephant has not taken place is northern Botswana – which has in fact seen the reverse. In the years between 1874 and 1879, Frederick Courteney Selous, the noted English hunter and naturalist, reported elephants across much of north-eastern Botswana. The elephant inevitably came under heavy hunting pressure and were scattered over a range extending into present-day Zimbabwe, Caprivi in the north, and Zambia. Dr. Graham Child, while a consultant to the F.A.O. of the United Nations, noted in a 1968 report to the government of Botswana a build-up of the elephant populations of northern Botswana. He placed the total at some 16 000 elephants. By contrast, an estimate by biologist George Calef, on contract to the Botswana Department of Wildlife and National Parks, put the population at approximately 50 000 elephants in the late 1980s – an enormous increase from the days of Selous, and even since Child's estimate.

The open range of these elephants extends from the Okavango Delta east through the Chobe National Park and clear across to the west side of Zimbabwe.

Savuti, within the Chobe National Park, comprises a large marsh adjacent to the fossil lake bed known as the Mababe Depression. A series of hills including Gubatsaa and Gcoha rims the northern side of the marsh and the Magwikhwe sand ridge, cut by the Savuti Channel, runs along the western side. Savuti is home to a large concentration of elephants, come dry times or good times.

And both do come. In the not quite 150 years covered by the historical record of the area, the Savuti Channel has had highly erratic flow. David Livingstone found water in Lake Ngami, to the south of the Okavango Delta, in 1849 and when he crossed the Savuti with his wife and children in the 1850s the water in the channel was a metre deep and some thirty-six metres wide. But by 1879 when Selous saw the channel, it was bone dry. The hunter A. G. Stigand found the channel dry in the early 1920s, and claimed that it had been so since the 1880s.

Savuti bulls of the seep.

In spite of a heavy flood year in 1925, the Savuti remained dry. Bobby Wilmot recorded that the channel began flowing again by 1957-58 to cease in 1966, and resume flowing into the Savuti marsh again in 1967. By 1969 the water had formed a great lake covering many square kilometres in the Mababe Depression. This heart-shaped basin, some ninety kilometres long and fifty kilometres wide, is a low-lying sump fed from the north by waters emerging from the Savuti marsh – when the channel pours enough water into the marsh. And then in 1981-82, the channel started drying up again.

As the waters of the channel retreated, most of the hippo and crocodile finally gave up living in mud holes and moved upstream toward the Linyanti swamp. But three crocodiles we found, one of which was a metre and a half long, holed up in some caves in the Gcoha Hills at Savuti. They held out during the dry season and moved into the numerous pans around Savuti during the rains, and then with the onset of the next dry season moved back into the caves.

We clambered in on our bellies to see how they were faring. Two disappeared after the second season but the largest stuck it out, to succumb only after more than eighteen months. We presumed they fed on what they could catch in the pans. They often shared a mud hole or pan with the odd hippo and had to evade the elephants that daily gathered for a drink. The water was foul-smelling to say the least, and the crocodiles had no choice but to tolerate the Savuti elephant bulls.

I first went to Savuti with an American university expedition in 1978. We drove from the Chobe River to Savuti and stayed beside the clear waters of the channel at the public campsite. The numbers of elephants, the stately camel thorn woodland and the vast array of wildlife attracted to the marsh made a powerful impression on me. There were enormous concentrations of buffalo and their dust could be observed for miles as they made their way toward the marsh, closely followed by the ever-present lions. Later P. J. Besterlink in the Okavango introduced me to Lloyd Wilmot, his brother-in-law, who had set up a home on the banks of the Savuti Channel. Born in 1947, Lloyd is the only son of the late Bobby Wilmot.

Bobby had started hunting crocodiles in 1956 and for the next thirteen years he and his assistants shot thousands of crocodiles up and down the Okavango, the Boteti, Thamalakane and Nhabe rivers, and the Thaoge and Xudum rivers on the west side of the Okavango. Bobby had known every waterway of this great system. The longest crocodile he shot measured more than five metres

Darter.

'*morotomadi*'
Kiaat

(sixteen feet, seven inches) and was taken on the Boteti River where their presence is unheard of today. In 1968 Bobby died from the effects of a snakebite after landing his boat on the edge of Ikoga lagoon. He injected himself with snakebite serum and then set off to get help at Sepopa village, some twenty kilometres away, but succumbed in the arms of his assistant. That snake ended the life of one of the most interesting and adventurous men ever to wander the length and breadth of Ngamiland.

Bobby took Lloyd to the Okavango in 1957. It was Bobby's second crocodile hunting season, and Lloyd went with him at age ten up the Boro channel. The following year Lloyd shot his first crocodile near the Chobe River. Lloyd took up crocodile hunting in earnest after he left school and shot over a thousand crocodiles during his short hunting career. In recent years I have come to know Lloyd very well – so well that I was his best man when he married June Anthony in 1986, and when their son Ashley arrived I became the child's godfather.

June joined Lloyd as a camp assistant straight from England in March 1981, on a recommendation from a friend, and has been there ever since. The camp is also home to honey badgers which patrol the place nightly like domestic dogs. By day the camp is a farmyard of hornbills, francolin, tree squirrels, baboons, vervet monkeys, occasional lions and numerous elephants that drink from the water hole Lloyd has built next to his camp in the dry Savuti Channel.

Honey Badgers can be a scourge in camp. Once when I was in the Savuti lion research camp with Brian Walker, then professor in the Department of Botany at the University of the Witwatersrand, our pilot Peter Joffe, and Neo Moroka, biologist in the Botswana Department of Wildlife, we had an episode with one. After a long day we retired to bed, Peter and I in one tent and Neo and Brian in the other. Neo, very definitely the city type, zipped the sides on their tent up completely, whereas Peter and I left ours wide open. Soon after falling asleep Peter and I were woken by a terrific crashing from the kitchen area. It sounded as if the camp was under attack. Silence fell back upon the night and when no further commotion took place, we dozed off to sleep.

The next morning upon checking the kitchen we discovered that a honey badger had somehow forced the wooden table that had been wedged across the opening and, standing on its hind legs, had reached up and opened the gas stove door, which it then climbed upon. The stove, top-heavy with cooking pots, was tipped by the weight of the badger. The resulting din was enormous, and no doubt the badger got a considerably worse shock than we did. When he emerged, Neo announced that he had had a wonderful night's sleep and had heard nothing. Brian looked as if he hadn't slept all night.

Many people have had memorable experiences with Lloyd Wilmot. He has an uncanny affinity with wildlife, and seems not to know fear – which sometimes causes his family some concern. But he seems blessed with a charmed life and his exploits are legend. He once accompanied me on a trail in the Savuti and one evening we heard the death bellow of a buffalo. Dark was falling as we set off armed with torches to look for the lions we presumed to be responsible. Lloyd wanted to see where they were and how many lions there were in the group. They were very close to camp, judging from the sounds of the dying buffalo.

In the gathering gloom he and I were making our way over there when Lloyd suddenly dropped to his knees and I did likewise. Staring ahead, he pointed out a mass of shapes surrounding the now silent buffalo. It was a large group of lions, by now busily tearing at the lifeless form.

Suddenly Lloyd snapped on his flashlight and there, not five metres away, was a crouching lioness. She had detected our presence, was not at all happy with our intrusion, and had come to investigate. Lloyd's light caused her to lie flat on the ground and he told me to keep my light on her face. He then spun his torch around and there was a second lion, this one a male, looking equally interested in our presence. I recall feeling very uncomfortable.

How do we get out of here? I wondered, trusting all the while in Lloyd's ability to effect our escape. Sure enough, he had an idea. We began moving on our knees, back to back, fending off

each lion's advances by waving our flashlights as ominously as possible. It took us at least fifteen minutes to retreat, kneeling often on the sharp thorns of the camel thorn twigs scattered on the ground. Try walking on your knees without the aid of your hands in soft Kalahari sand. It's an experience you will not forget, even if you are not accompanied by lions.

After we had moved back about a hundred metres, the lions lost interest. We gathered up our tattered wits and headed for camp, only to walk into a lone bull elephant. We crouched down and he halted, turned, and with arched back which we could plainly see in the light of a rising moon, slowly stalked around us before disappearing silently into the gloom.

Thousands of visitors from around the globe have by now experienced Savuti's cold midwinter dawns on early morning game drives; the roar of lions; and, before 1982, the sight of thousands of buffalo, their dust column visible long before they reached the channel. Still to be seen are some 20 000 zebra which pass through at the start of the rains and then again when the rainy season ends.

This was where I watched a lone roan antelope bull, motionless at the edge of a pan in dust swirling from the August winds, his strong horns curving back, snorting at the antics of bull elephants shoving each other about at the water's edge. There are the bateleur eagles, wings rocking to and fro as they patrol the Savuti skies, free and untroubled by poison. Kori bustards stalk the marsh, always keeping a discreet distance from safari vehicles. Hyaena, jackal, honey badger, cheetah, leopard, wild dogs and a host of other creatures live here. This was where I first swam among elephants and watched from a tree platform overlooking a bend in the channel as they drank and bathed.

In the dry, harsh, burnt landscape at the end of winter, game stands listlessly; elephant fight more frequently. October brings the heat and high thunder clouds rise majestically above the golden grass-covered marsh. At last, the rains come in November and December. The pans fill and the elephants disperse. The change in vegetation is dramatic and tourist numbers drop to a trickle. The long-awaited summer rains restore life to Savuti.

Early man lived here too and left rock paintings on the Gubatsaa Hills as a reminder that Savuti was his home long before we arrived with our technological arrogance. Harsh and cruel it may seem at times, but Savuti was a safe haven for many creatures until recently. In July of 1989 poachers killed four large bull elephants in the

Chobe. The carcasses of three elephants were found by over-flying pilots and then in early August, Peter Hitchins and I stayed at Lloyd's camp and learned of the killing. Flying over the park, we found the fourth one.

Hitchins and I took a hike to see the carcasses of the poached elephants. It's always difficult to look at dead elephants – somehow their very size seems to make their deaths more of a sadness than death is anyway. Their great skulls, hacked and chopped, silently berated us. As we walked, searching for the dead bulls, we were following an ancient elephant path, a narrow well-beaten track between pans. Signs of elephant were everywhere – camel thorn trees ringbarked or pushed down.

It was the smell that led us to the carcasses, and we could see that other elephants had been inspecting those carcasses before us. Are elephants nowhere safe? Is it too much to hope that Savuti, at least, will forever be a place of elephants?

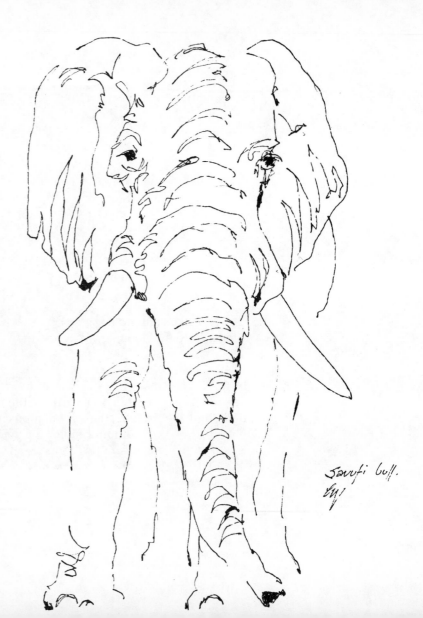

Savuti bull.

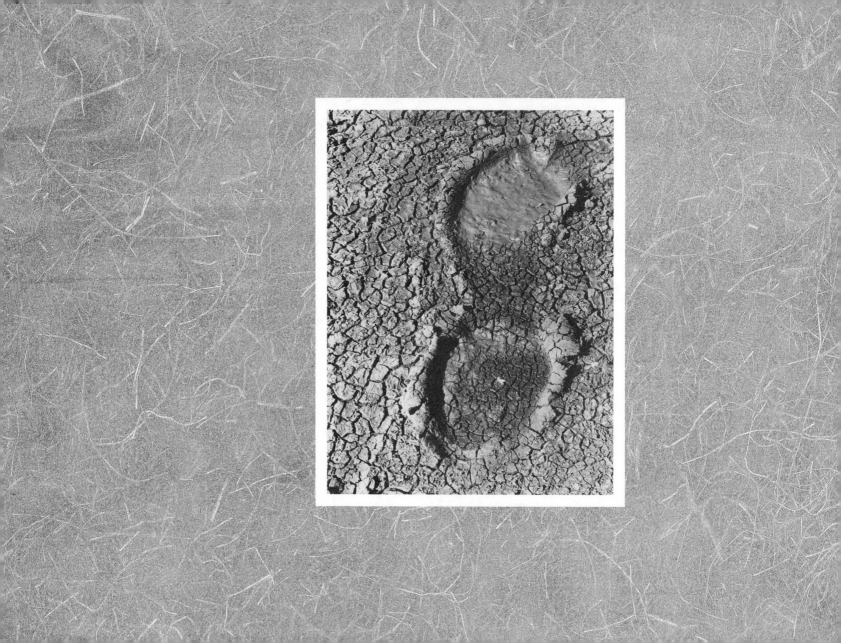

13.
Silent Desert

Nine million hectares of wilderness in the far north of Namibia; nine million hectares of pristine wild country, the likes of which exist nowhere else in southern Africa. After more than forty years of stability as a tribal reserve and game reserve, suddenly war, depredation, politics, the greed of a few and the ignorance of many intruded upon the scene in this land in 1970. Damaraland and Kaokoland are the two political regions that comprise the Kaokoveld, a unique part of Africa.

Dr Anton Rupert announced in *African Wildlife* magazine in 1976, "As President of the Southern African Nature Foundation, I am glad to be able to tell you that the Prime Minister of South Africa has just informed me of one of the most important events in the history of nature conservation. A contiguous nature conservation area covering 72 000 square kilometres is being planned for the northern part of South West Africa. This allays many fears which scientists of the International Union for the Conservation of Nature and Natural Resources and the World Wildlife Fund have had, as regards the future of this important habitat. This conservation area will include the existing Etosha Game Reserve as well as the Skeleton Coast Park and will be more than three times the size of the Kruger National Park and indeed one of the largest in the world."

rhino horn

The sad fact was that most of the black rhino in the region had been poached, the elephant had fared little better, and the ravages of a five-year drought were to leave their mark. But few people knew what was going on there. The public were banned from entry as the Kaokoveld had been under the control of the South African government's Department of Bantu Affairs. My first visit was in 1978 at the invitation of Professor Koos Bothma and Professor Fritz Eloff, both of the University of Pretoria. They were engaged in a study of the Kaokoveld and were among a handful of people who were worried about the wildlife there. Another concerned party was Garth Owen-Smith, who had once worked there but had become a ranger in Etosha National Park. They knew things were dreadfully wrong. The Kaokoveld was in effect a private hunting preserve for a privileged few in official positions, and it was so sparsely populated that the authorities could not hope to police it against poaching. War in Angola meant that firearms, including automatic weapons, were available in northern Namibia, and it meant a South African Defence Force presence in the Kaokoveld.

It was arranged that I would meet Fritz and Koos near the Namibia/Angola border in a valley known as the Marienfluss, not far from the Kunene River. At my own expense, the Endangered Wildlife Trust was not as yet involved, I flew from Johannesburg to Windhoek where a young architect had been lined up by Koos to fly me to the Kaokoveld. I wanted to see for myself the place of which Fritz and Koos spoke so highly, and which they loved so much, and hoped later to persuade the Trust to enter the picture, although at the time I had no idea how. Elephants were not endangered continent-wide and rhino in 1978 numbered in the tens of thousands. Yet in the 1970s there had been a major decline in Kaokoveld elephant numbers, because of the combined depredations of ivory poachers on the one hand, and prominent politicians and government officials on the other.

Our plane started a slow descent toward the Marienfluss, which runs in a south-north direction with steep mountains on the east side. Koos remarked later that they heard our aircraft for some time but failed to pick it out in the vast landscape. There is something about its emptiness that reduces human things to nearly nothing.

Rows of empty aircraft fuel drums lay about and the old marks of a desert landing strip were visible. This was it, right out in the middle of nowhere and only a few kilometres from the Angolan border. Then we picked out a large truck, a South African Defence Force Unimog. The army had provided our party with an escort of two young men to accompany us back south through the Kaokoveld; a low intensity bush war was the reason for the caution. We refuelled the Cessna 172, loaded my equipment into Koos's truck and soon were watching the aircraft heading south for Windhoek. My Kaokoveld journey had begun.

We spent the afternoon filming the Ovahimba, desert-dwelling pastoralist people who live on the eastern edge of the northern highlands. The following day we headed south across the gravel flats, looking for rhino and elephant. We bade Koos farewell at a remote T-junction, he was to return to Windhoek and see about some vehicle problems. As we watched his dust rising we saw a vehicle approaching him from the direction in which he was heading, where there was a well-known fountain in the desert. We were to find out later that it had been a police vehicle. The police stopped Koos as they said they were checking on poaching activities. In departing from the spring they had left a good deal of rubbish lying around their still smouldering fire. Fritz shook his head in disgust at the insensitive attitudes of people who came into such areas in total ignorance and saw nothing wrong in leaving litter about.

A day later we came upon our first black rhino carcass near a fountain. The animal had been shot as it came to drink. We found numerous ele-

phant carcasses as we progressed further south and another rhino. Fritz was infuriated that this hunting had been conducted by people who had no idea of the significance of the creatures that inhabited this amazing place whether those hunters were civil servants abusing their positions to shoot for pleasure, or poachers who shot purely for profit. It was not surprising that most of the big game species had declined dramatically.

We finally saw our first live desert elephants near the Hoanib River, three bulls, and we spent a number of hours filming them. The Hoanib divides Damaraland from Kaokoland. That day in the Hoanib River, I made my mind up that we, the EWT, must address the problem as an organisation. Here were rhinos and elephants distinctively adapted to life in a harsh, dry wilderness, and they were simply being slaughtered.

The first thing I did was write a report which I sent to the International Union for the Conservation of Nature in Switzerland, the Southern African Nature Foundation (SANF), and the South African government. A copy was also sent to the Administrator of South West Africa.

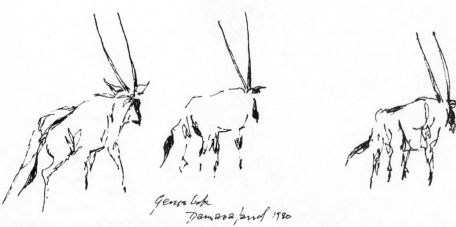

*Gemsbok
Damaraland 1980*

Next I submitted to *African Wildlife* an article entitled "Who is doing the killing now?" Among other things, that piece had this to say: "Until a year (ago), the Kaokoveld was closed to all, bar government officials. No member of the public could go in without a permit and permits were rarely if ever given. Persistent rumours of poaching in the area came to a head in July 1977 when a press investigation revealed that officials in high places had been hunting elephant as well as the rare black-faced impala."

"During the controversy a Windhoek reporter was sentenced to a jail term for refusing to disclose his sources of information (his conviction was set aside on appeal). Meanwhile a senior nature conservation official from the Department of Bantu Affairs claimed that he was transferred out of the territory after querying the shooting of elephant. A Windhoek newspaper was about to publish a 16 000-word 'calm, cool, factual story of game dying' when the Defence Force froze further newspaper reports, and set up an inquiry into some of the allegations.

"The Administrator General of South West Africa/Namibia, Mr. Justice M. T. Steyn, promised to take drastic action to protect the territory's wildlife, and he mentioned the Kaokoveld as a possible future reserve. He organised a meeting with nature conservation authorities to discuss the future of wildlife but the Kaokoveld continued to be the target of illegal hunters."

Garth Owen-Smith and renowned South African wildlife scientist Ken Tinley had both sounded early warnings about the Kaokoveld but neither worked or had any influence in the region any longer. Both men had produced important reports which had gone largely unnoticed. Fritz and Koos were in the final stages of a study for a master plan for the Kaokoveld; a decade later, this too was only gathering dust. My report was not a study. It was an alarm note, and it was not long before the South African Defence Force contacted me. Soon after, I found myself in the office of a certain General Lemmer, responsible for conservation.

It is true to say the SADF had in those days a very bad public image when it came to conservation matters and northern Namibia was no exception. I did my best to point out what we believed was taking place and they undertook to look into the situation. They tried to point out to me that the Defence Force was in fact very anxious to maintain the wildlife in the areas under its control and did not condone the slaughter. Many conservationists were not too convinced about that. But the Endangered Wildlife Trust decided to establish closer links with General Lemmer's depart-

ment and as a consequence of the meeting built up an excellent relationship which eventually led to establishment of the EWT annual trophy for the best conservation accomplishments among military units. The SADF conservation record today is outstanding and I derive no small measure of satisfaction from having been part of that effort. At one time I would have been only too happy to have seen the perpetrators of inroads against wildlife brought down, but in this case a more lasting positive effect was achieved by endeavouring to help in a constructive way. Individuals within that system who had abused their positions of authority to destroy desert wildlife now had to become accountable.

The next step was to get some more systematic work going in the Kaokoveld. Ernst Taeuber, an SANF board member with business interests in Namibia, arranged a dinner in Windhoek of influential business people and conservationists to highlight the need to conserve the desert fauna. Koos Bothma and I discussed the need for the study University of Pretoria researcher "Slang" Viljoen was to commence the following year on the elephant, rhino and giraffe. I had by now convinced the EWT to finance aerial surveys over the next two years and thus began our full involvement in the Kaokoveld. Koos had meanwhile been put in touch with Ina and Colin Britz who worked for Consolidated Diamond Mines stationed in Damaraland at a camp known as Wêreldsend. This was to become our base for five years and Ina and Colin greatly eased our way.

Colin was a prospector for CDM and his knowledge of both Damaraland and Kaokoland was extensive. When flying in such a vast uninhabited area, having a reliable ground base is essential. EWT trustee Peter Joffe piloted us in his Mooney four-seater which enabled us to keep operating costs down. The next two years saw Slang and Peter, with an assortment of observers, cover thousands of kilometres across the Kaokoveld in search of rhino and elephant. Dr. Anthony Hall-Martin, black rhino specialist Peter Hitchins and I subsequently carried out a further survey in search of black rhino.

While theoretically easier than ground surveys, aerial work offers its share of problems too.

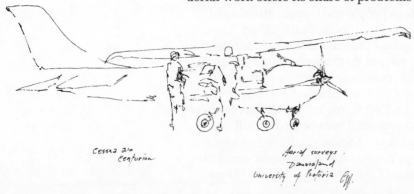

Cessna 210
Centurion

Aerial surveys.
Damaraland
University of Pretoria

Returning from the Kaokoveld during February 1983 after spending the better part of five days dodging heavy rain, thunder and lightning, we had climbed bumpily out of Windhoek's Eros Airport and headed out for the Nossob River and home across the vast expanse of the Kalahari desert. In the plane were Angus Morrison, then chairman of EWT, pilot Peter Joffe, and in the rear Peter Hitchins and I. Hitchins and I dozed off.

Peter Joffe had observed hazy weather up ahead but could not know that behind the haze was a huge thunder cloud which rose up thousands of feet. We steamed straight into this and were instantly very wide awake and knocked about violently, hitting our heads repeatedly on the ceiling. Visibility was absolutely nil. Clutching the seats in front, Hitchins and I watched in fascination as the altimeter reeled off the feet of our swift climb. Peter had the aircraft stable with all the power off and we travelled at a speed of 140 knots not forward but *upward* at 3 000 feet per minute with full flaps, gear down and the motor chopped, for a full five minutes.

Aerial surveys clearly revealed the extent of the poaching and the urgent need for action to save the rhino and elephant. During our second year, Ina together with Blythe Loutit had the idea of forming a wildlife trust in Namibia and set about establishing what became the Namibian Wildlife

Trust, with considerable assistance from Consolidated Diamond Mines. The Endangered Wildlife Trust, after our two-year initial research project undertaken by Koos Bothma's Eugene Marais Chair of Wildlife Management, came in behind Ina's Trust with financial assistance, at my request, which enabled them to employ Garth Owen-Smith, who was very happy to leave Etosha at the prospect of working in the Kaokoveld. Garth was an obvious choice for such a position and has proven to be one of the mainstays in the reversing of the downward spiral of the desert rhino and elephant.

It was not however an easy path. At the time the Damaras were fiercely divided over the government's role: although they were ostensibly governed directly from Pretoria (which gave them control over the wildlife), the territory itself was administered by second tier (Windhoek) government. We were caught in the middle because both felt threatened by our continuing exposure of the extent of illegal killing. Thanks to the findings of our surveys, I was soon a target for criticism. Our funding was acceptable but it was clear that we weren't expected to voice too many opinions. The more we revealed the extent of the poaching the greater the embarrassment to those in charge. The subsequent killing of a desert research elephant by a safari concession client, while legal, gave us a dramatic opportunity to draw attention to the plight of the rhino and elephant. Blythe Loutit flew to Cape Town and saw the Minister of Environment Affairs and I went on television. The public outcry was considerable. Windhoek became more and more agitated and embarrassed.

As more support came our way, I flew wildlife artist Paul Bosman up to Wêreldsend on one trip with Fritz and Koos. Paul's resulting painting of desert elephants enabled us to raise over R40 000 for the Kaokoveld. On that particular trip Fritz, Paul and I spent one day in a nearby valley known as Palm. The remains of a farm house indicated where settlers had once lived and a clear spring still gave out a steady stream near what had been a sheep kraal. Here we found a family of cow and calf elephants drinking and rolling in the mud. We followed the elephant for several hours at a discreet distance, taking photographs. We watched them venture out onto the bare, jagged rock ever so slowly, and make their way along ancient foot paths, shuffling loose boulders out of the way. The beautiful mauve and purple mountains rose above us on either side as we slowly made our way into the valley.

What manner of person, I thought, would seek to come here and blast the life out of such special creatures that had learned to survive in such a hostile world? As we made our way further into

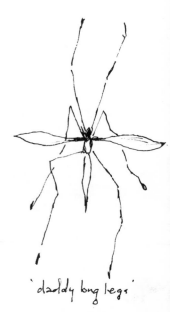

'daddy long legs'

this world and the temperature rose, the family group of eleven took up a position in a grove of mopane trees on an island in a dry stone gully. Paul remained on the bank as Fritz and I went in for a closer look. Both of us being ardent photographers, we were somewhat over-enthusiastic and were soon spotted or perhaps heard by the cows. They had been hunted, and were showing signs of alarm.

Before we could retreat in an orderly way, the largest cow, an impressive matriarch with a badly broken ear, charged out screaming. She first saw Fritz, who had been standing next to a mopane tree. I was ten or fifteen feet behind him and seeing Fritz turn to run, she went for him like an express train. I ran for the bank where Paul was standing as Fritz passed me at a dead run. I remember his arms pumping up and down and gaze fixed dead ahead and needed no word of encouragement to get out of this. As I took off, I knocked the metal lens cap off my camera. It clattered on the stones in the river bed and this caused her to stop, see me, and turn in my direction, leaving Fritz to make good his flight which he continued to do for about five hundred metres. I in the meantime effected my own escape up the steep bank. The cow stood below grumbling (that is the best way I can explain the sound coming from her throat) until satisfied that she had chased us off. In her charge she was fol-

lowed by a number of her group, which milled around her now as they made their way back into the thick mopane.

Fritz and I had been charged on a previous occasion when we had got too close to a one-eyed bull elephant in the Hoanib River back in 1978. Fritz was behind me that time and when the bull charged I ran up a steep dune toward Fritz with the elephant behind me. Fritz was busy taking pictures with a 400 mm zoom lens and the view he must have got caused him to abandon all further photography and take off on the double with me trying to keep up. It's not surprising that he achieved Springbok colours for rugby as a young man.

One aerial survey found us based away from Wêreldsend. This particular expedition included an exercise by Koos Bothma's department to immobilise a large desert elephant bull and fit him with a radio collar which would enable them to track his movements. We had set up camp on the upper reaches of the Hoanib south of Sesfontein, a tiny outpost lying between Damaraland and Kaokoveld. We had a superb camp under large *Acacia albida* trees and on a return flight in search of a suitable elephant bull we noticed a carcass in the river course. We quickly landed our aircraft and immediately set off in search of the carcass.

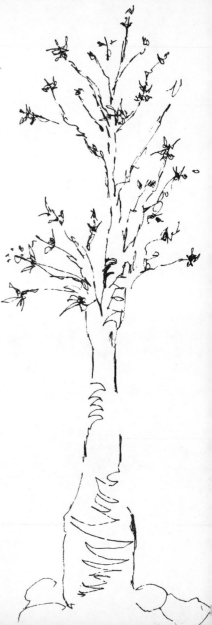

It was near noon and hot as we drove less than a kilometer from camp and there, lying mummified in the sand, were the remains of a bull elephant minus his ivory. It did not take long to find three more elephants, this time cows, also minus their ivory. They all appeared to have been shot in close proximity to each other. As we were to observe, when alarmed these elephants would bunch up and mill around inside thickets and they could easily be picked off as they revealed a head or shoulder. We stood in silence in that hot river bed.

In death they appeared to be sleeping. Much of the skin still remained. We detected no smell coming from these mummified creatures. It was as if we had uncovered an elephant tomb. It all seemed so pointless. Here we were looking all day for a live elephant and instead in our midst lay four dead ones. Little did we realise there were three more dead elephants less than five kilometres away on the north side of the Hoanib River. This time chainsaws had been used to remove the ivory and the slugs of automatic weapons lay within the remains.

Garth went on to establish a conservation network of auxiliary game guards among local people and this has proven invaluable in assisting the authorities in anti-poaching efforts. By 1983 poaching had mainly been brought under control. First funded by the Namibian Wildlife Trust and then by the Endangered Wildlife Trust, the work was taken over at the end of 1984 by the Directorate of Nature Conservation, with EWT continuing to support the programme financially. Much has been achieved and many organisations and individuals have made important contributions and continue to do so.

I suppose it was inevitable that after leaving the Endangered Wildlife Trust, I would be drawn back toward work involving the desert elephants, this time through the Rhino and Elephant Foundation. We are as yet no closer to the Prime Minister's long ago promise of a 72 000-square kilometre conservation area in the Kaokoveld, and there is work to be done. I have flown many thousands of kilometres in search of rhino and elephant over the most breathtaking country but the Kaokoveld will forever be the most enchanting – the silent desert, with its hidden secrets, beautifully coloured mountains rising sheer out of the gravel flats, and wonderful people who have fought so hard to ensure its long-term conservation.

14.
Creatures of Discontent

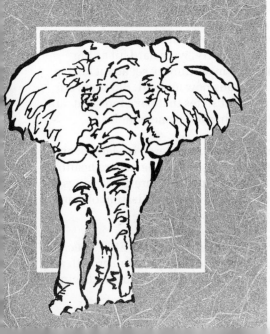

It would be humbug of me to pretend that I didn't enjoy the high profile aspect of my work running the Endangered Wildlife Trust. It was certainly the most important and demanding job I had ever held. The work was much more than mere administration. It gave me the opportunity to get out into the open a lot and to visit other countries in Africa and abroad. It provided me with a continuing education in wildlife conservation.

It called for fund-raising involving many thousands of rands; it required constant publicity to keep the aims of the EWT before the public eye and, in this, my training in an advertising agency proved useful. It was important to maintain a high public profile and I soon discovered I had an aptitude for this. My relations with the media were good and the EWT benefitted from wide and regular coverage of many meetings, press conferences and public appearances. I took pleasure in talking about our work, especially when it resulted in donations and bequests from people who had heard me on the subject of endangered wildlife and who were won over to help in a positive way. Money was our lifeline and I shall always be grateful for the generosity of our benefactors.

The work also entailed getting out into the field in order to supervise our programmes and to maintain a watchful eye on the research being undertaken.

We were spending money given to us by others and it was important to ensure that none of it was misspent or wasted on anything but the vital work of saving endangered animals from extinction. The EWT began its work in South Africa and Botswana, extended its activities to Namibia, and has remained deeply involved in all three countries as well as embarking on work in war-torn Mozambique. Political considerations have reduced and, in many cases, eliminated contact in other parts of the subcontinent. Many years ago I learned to accept the inevitability of change, especially in Africa; *ex Africa semper nove.*

But the desire for change is strictly a people thing. I have come to believe that discontent is, basically, what distinguishes people from other beings. A mammal, bird or reptile population, given sufficient food sources and shelter, could remain in one spot for centuries; animals' needs are constant and immutable. We alone nurture the seed of discontent in our bosom and it is in our nature to seek implacably for what we regard as better things.

So it is with our continent. The changes in Africa since World War II are regarded by some as ill-considered, premature, or both. People point to famines, internecine wars, massive corruption and the tyrannies that have characterised the transition to African independence, as though these prove something. As far as I am concerned, they prove only that the world and its people never stand still. For better or for worse, discontent breeds change and there is little we can do to halt the universal process. We can but hope to guide it.

There is no denying that the fauna of Africa has been a major casualty in this shifting upheaval. Many emergent governments placed wildlife conservation low on their list of priorities and this, too, is understandable. Conservation laws were inherited from the colonialists and they were either swept aside or ignored. Animal populations suffered grievously in many cases. Elephant and rhino, particularly, were hard hit as the poachers and the meat-hungry set about killing them with weapons new and old. But there are some independent states that have foresight and plain good sense in their game policies.

Zimbabwe is a good example; so is Malawi; and so, above all others, is Botswana, where healthy wildlife populations provide foreign earnings through tourism, and where utilisation of game is a significant source of protein.

During my last four years with the EWT I became increasingly interested in population growth and the over-utilisation of natural resources, beginning to understand the ways that exist to safeguard our natural heritage against waste and undue exploitation. I found myself crossing people on a number of controversial matters concerning wildlife conservation. By some academics I was regarded as a maverick who lacked scientific background yet dared to argue with them on topics in their own field. I upset some, irritated some, infuriated others and earned the opprobrium of quite a few. But I also made many true friends who backed me in a number of ways. And in due course I learned lessons, both painful and salutary. I discovered that the conservation world, despite its aura of altruism, is by no means free of the petty jealousies that beset other organisations both public and private. It has its quota of prima donnas wary of anyone standing between themselves and the first available spotlight and I tended to be in the limelight.

When I left the EWT, these factors played a part in my decision. But I must hasten to add that they were the minor ones. My main reasons for leaving were twofold. I had been given the opportunity to manage and develop the Lapalala Wilderness game reserve in the Waterberg, which required more time than I could give it unless I left the Trust. The second reason was the realisation that conservation is and will always remain a people business.

On the face of it, this seems obvious enough. Nothing can be done for protection of wildlife without active involvement by men and women, and the money they supply in both the public and the private sectors. Yet I firmly believe that conservation must cease to be the preserve of wealthy enthusiasts, no matter how well-intentioned they may be. These people have played an invaluable role in maintaining the conservation movement and one must always be grateful for their generosity and far-sightedness. But today the problem of conserving natural resources has become universal. It involves everybody, even those who have never seen a wild animal especially those, since it is they and their children who may one day be left with no earth to inherit.

On a visit to India some years ago I was immensely impressed by the fact that, despite the enormity of India's problems in trying to find food and employment for her millions of dispossessed and impoverished, her government nevertheless found the means to establish sanctuaries for the Indian tiger and the Asian rhino. India is saving these animals because she is committed to this task in a way that Africa still has to learn to do. Why can't the countries of Africa do the same?

In a place like Soweto, with its estimated two million inhabitants, there are a mere handful of

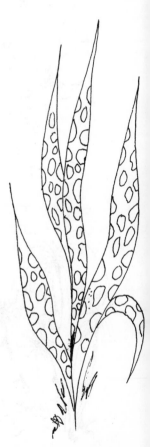

Silver leaf.

children who have ever been further than a ten-kilometre radius from their homes. The vast majority of the urban blacks of South Africa had forebears just four or five generations ago who lived in and on the African bush; who hunted kudu and eland; who grazed their cattle along the plains of Zululand and the Transvaal; who survived because of their affinity with their natural surroundings. But today these people have not the slightest awareness of the bushveld. They have scarcely encountered a forest or a plain or a river or a pan. They know wildlife mainly through folklore and this is fast disappearing. Most of Soweto's young people have never even paid a visit to the Johannesburg zoo.

Obviously the socio-economic and political factors which govern their lives are responsible for this parlous state of affairs. There is little conservationists can do about this except as concerned citizens. But what we can and must do is introduce as many black youngsters as possible to the mysteries of the wild world that exists beyond the shacks and ditches of Daveyton and Orlando and the other overcrowded townships which dot our country. It was to this aim, of thus exposing all children who grow up in the cities, that I and a handful of friends dedicated ourselves. My priorities had changed. It was now time to help as many people as possible to experience and understand a wild environment. Trailing

achieves this to some degree, but a wilderness school focuses matters better yet.

The vast majority of people on this planet are supremely unconcerned with saving the cheetah or any other animal from extinction. They cannot understand why conservationists are so anxious to protect the elephant of the Kaokoveld or northern Botswana or Zululand. They are unmoved and indifferent to the fate of the rhino, black or white. This is particularly true of people living on the edge of hunger and deprivation. Even the broader issue of conserving the environment is non-existent on their list of priorities for reasons that are not hard to fathom. When their needs are so great, the subject seems fanciful and idealistic. Does this mean there is nothing we can do until living conditions have materially improved?

I do not believe so. It has been my experience that those black people of this country with whom I have been in contact respond very readily to a rational programme of education in conservation. The young men and women who have come on some of our courses have responded magnificently to what they have learned. They have shown all the keenness and enthusiasm of their white companions, and in some cases more.

My introduction to Lapalala was an accident. Having failed to establish a trailing operation in the Pilanesberg National Park, I was directed to Lapalala by Val Ford through a friend of hers who knew the owner, ex-Kenya big game hunter Eric Rundgren. Eric gave us a three-month option to purchase the farm for just over half a million rand, an awful lot of money in those days. After two and a half months of fund-raising, the five of us, Harry Boots, Dawie Botha, Peter Joffe, John Young, and I had each put five thousand rand into a trust account to secure the necessary deposit, but purchase still seemed a remote goal.

Meanwhile, I was involved in a two-day survey to count the elephants in the Knysna forest. EWT trustee Dale Parker of Cape Town offered to fly Dr. Tony Hall of the Bolus Herbarium at the University of Cape Town up to Knysna to assist us. After completing the survey (wherein it was established that only three elephants inhabited the forest), we all set off to Knysna for dinner. Considerable discussion took place during the course of the meal about this place called Lapalala in the Waterberg Mountains. Keith Cooper from the Wildlife Society, who also knew Eric Rundgren, had visited the area and remarked upon its magnificence and its wide diversity of plant life.

That must have made the right impression, because the following morning when I took Dale and Tony to the Knysna airstrip for their return

Lapalala Wilderness
Roan bull
GW.

flight to Cape Town, Dale called me aside after the pre-flight check. "If I were to consider buying the farm, would you be prepared to manage and develop it with me?" he inquired. Two things had impressed him immensely: the possibility of roan antelope roaming these mountains again, and the beautiful stretch of the Lephalala River, which I had described so enthusiastically. It would also give me the opportunity of setting up the environmental school that I had so long wished to establish.

I flew back to Johannesburg excited at the prospect that we might, in the last moments of the option, really be able to acquire the farm. I obtained an extension of time from Eric, and Sandy and John Eastwood accompanied Dale and his wife Libby, as they had in 1979 when I guided them on a five-day wilderness trail in the Okavango, to see Lapalala. It is extraordinary how friendships are established as a result of wilderness trailing. The trip also included lawyer Dawie Botha, a trustee of the Wilderness Trust. It took just one afternoon for Dale and Libby to make up their minds, after I had taken them to a high rocky outcrop known as Lepotedi, which in the local dialect refers to the blue-headed agama. As they gazed down, I knew that the wheels had been set in motion for the purchase of Lapalala Wilderness.

Over the past eleven years, the reserve has increased in size from its original five thousand hectares up to its present 24 400 hectares, one of the largest sanctuaries in South Africa with a single owner, and the first private reserve to acquire black rhinoceros. In June 1990, Natal Parks Board made history by auctioning a founder population of black rhino, two bulls and three cows, for which Dale Parker successfully bid R2,2 million, the highest price ever paid for the species. That August the five rhino were translocated to special holding pens within Lapalala Wilderness, the first black rhino to be seen in this mountain range for 150 years, if not longer.

Besides providing the Natal Parks Board with important funding for its conservation programmes, this auction had considerable significance from a legal point of view, as well as establishing the substantial economic value of black rhino. Lapalala was one of eight private reserves considered suitable for black rhino introduction, based on assessments by Natal Parks Board representative Atholl Marchant and rhino specialist Peter Hitchins. I was on record as having said: "This is a great responsibility for us at Lapalala. The opportunity arises from the confidence the Natal Parks Board have placed in the private sector in allowing these animals to go onto private land. We are only too aware of what has happened to the black rhinoceros across Africa. Southern Africa is their last stronghold and we are happy to be part of their conservation. A great deal will be expected of us and we are going to have to measure up to those expectations."

Controversy surrounded the decision of the board to sell rhino to the private sector. Some within the conservation agencies in South Africa felt it was a mistake. Many questions remained unanswered. Was the private sector capable of looking after such an endangered species and were they prepared to spend sufficient funds to ensure their

protection? Possession is nine tenths of the law. Once the hammer fell and the price of R2,2 million was paid, no matter what was requested in terms of our not being allowed to resell the rhino or dispose of them as we wished, there was in reality little that the authorities could do.

Yet, who would argue that anyone who had the courage to spend such an enormous sum on living creatures which so easily could die within ten kilometres if they left the sanctuary, or if the transport vehicle conveying them to Lapalala were in an accident, would not take every precaution to ensure their protection and long-term survival? In the present economic climate, government agencies and conservation programmes have to face slashing and tightening up of budgets, and funding has to be sought elsewhere. The Natal Parks Board put up a further five rhino for auction in June of 1991. Whether the price of R2,2 million will ever be realised again seems doubtful, however. But we at Lapalala have been doing everything possible to ensure that the introduction of this highly endangered animal into these mountains is successful, and to date they have settled in extremely well. Time, of course, will tell if the decision taken by the Natal Parks Board was the right one.

For Dale Parker and me it was the right one. Apart from black rhino, species such as roan and

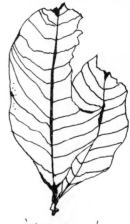

'lekkerbreek'

Bobbejaansterf

sable occur at Lapalala and there are two endangered species of fish, which occur in the more than sixty kilometres of the Lephalala River. A number of rare butterfly species and plants, as well as over three hundred species of birds also occur in the area. Together with an 18 000 ha. game reserve, Touchstone, owned by the Methven family and sharing an open boundary with Lapalala along the river, we have jointly formed the first nature conservancy in these mountains, totalling some 40 000 ha. in extent; it has the long-term potential of increasing up to some 150 000 ha. In little more than a decade, the habitat has shown good recovery from years of agricultural use.

The reserve has the enormous advantage of being only three hours by road from Johannesburg. At the beginning, game consisted only of kudu, small bands of wildebeest, baboons, a few impala, leopard and brown hyaena that had been heavily persecuted, and crocodiles in the Lephalala River. Since 1982, apart from the black rhino, there have been reintroductions of white rhino, giraffe, reedbuck, additional impala, tsessebe, sable, zebra, roan antelope, hippos, mongooses, and even owls and porcupines. It was with soaring spirits that we reintroduced three young elephants from the Kruger National Park in 1989, the first of several annual elephant introductions. This was followed by Touchstone

bringing in ten animals in 1990 and a further seven elephants being established in the reserve on our western boundary, Kwalata, which is essentially devoted to sport hunting.

The six bush camps in Lapalala are open all year and have proven to be so popular with visitors that they are fully booked within a month of bookings opening every September. When the concept for these camps was initiated in 1981, it was unique in the Transvaal: visitors checking in at reception were requested not to drive their motor vehicles after having driven to their respective camps. For the duration of their visit only walking, swimming and sightseeing were permitted. In essence, people were placed in trust within the game reserve. Over the decade that we have operated in the mountains, we have had very little abuse of that privilege, which I believe has major bearing upon Lapalala's focus of environmental education.

The Wilderness Trust, a non-profit, non-governmental organisation of which I am chairman, opened its first fully equipped field school in 1985 in what was a run-down farmhouse, and now accommodates seventy children at a time. Youth training in environmental subjects is a new field, only some twenty years old. There are others involved in this concept in various programmes in southern Africa – good, dedicated people. Like me, they also suffered discontent while working in related fields of conservation or education and gradually concluded that exposure of young people to wild places and creatures, with concurrent presentation of environmental needs, was the most important contribution they could make. I am grateful that I now have the opportunity to do this on a large scale. It is rewarding to conserve a small area of high ecological significance, and to participate in conserving populations of species that are in trouble like roan antelope and black rhinoceros. But it is a good deal more rewarding yet to know that young minds are being opened to the richness of the wilderness and to crucial environmental perspectives.

15.
Take a Glamorous Animal

The idea began to germinate in 1984, on the back of a Land Rover driven by Blythe Loutit in Damaraland. We were on a five-day visit to that part of the world and I had announced my resolve that it was time for me to step down as director of the Endangered Wildlife Trust. Concern was expressed by my two companions, Peter Hitchins and Anthony Hall-Martin, about the long-term future of rhinos and elephants. While both species were reasonably secure within South Africa, we were not yet confident of their status in Namibia, and elsewhere in Africa it was already clear that things were going from bad to worse. The Endangered Wildlife Trust had begun to expand its focus beyond "glamorous" animals, for the very good reason that as an organisation concerned with endangered species, it had a lot of wildlife to cover; a wide range of issues to address.

All three of us being intensely interested in rhinos and elephants, it was probably inevitable that we should move towards forming a body with these animals as its paramount concern. By 1986, despite our assorted other commitments, the prospect had really taken hold and the three of us began working seriously towards forming a group that would direct its attentions to the plight of rhinos and elephants. We considered becoming a working group affiliated to the EWT, but eventually decided to go it alone.

Thus the Rhino and Elephant Foundation came into being with Anthony Hall-Martin assuming the role of first chairman, and the Honourable M. G. Buthelezi, Chief Minister of KwaZulu, accepting the position of president. The REF was formally launched at a function at the Everard Read Gallery in Johannesburg, coinciding with a wildlife art exhibition; both Mark Read and his father, Everard, gave us their full support and blessing, and became trustees.

We never intended to launch an organisation that would be in competition with the established wildlife conservation bodies in South Africa, but hindsight reveals that we were being naive. Competition was unavoidable by virtue of the fact that one winds up competing for funds and for the backing of individuals and corporations. In this area the REF has faced its most severe critics.

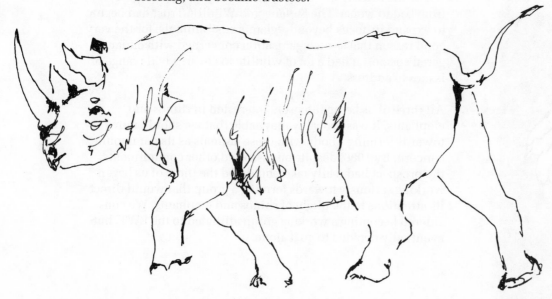

Black rhinoceros
Diceros bicornis bicornis

As a small, new organisation, REF was supported in spectacular style by that doyen of wildlife artists, David Shepherd. In a joint project with the Endangered Wildlife Trust and through the considerable efforts of Lucky Mavrandonis, a director of a Johannesburg-based pharmaceutical company and an EWT trustee, David agreed to travel to Kaokoland with Lucky, Everard Read, and EWT Director, John Ledger. The idea was to show David and Everard the famed Kaokoveld elephants, of which David had agreed to paint a picture, with a limited edition of prints to be published for sale in South Africa. The funds which were raised from the sale of these prints would be shared equally between EWT and REF.

David was insistent that I accompany the party. The trip, in 1988, was in a sense a triumphant return journey for me, for it brought me back into work involving the Kaokoveld. Returning there after an absence of nearly four years, and it was by then almost ten years since I had first gone there with Koos Bothma and Fritz Eloff, was cathartic. It was a long step from my first exposure to the atrocities against the desert fauna of that land to the systematic conservation work being conducted there by the late 1980s. The result of the venture was that some R300 000 was raised, of which R150 000 went to the Foundation and was subsequently applied to various projects within Damaraland and Etosha,

supporting both Blythe Loutit and the Etosha anti-poaching unit.

The Rhino and Elephant Foundation got under way in earnest thereafter and has since left no doubt that its existence is worthwhile. It has been extremely successful in drawing the plight of rhinos and elephants to the fore, sometimes so successful as to stand accused of undignified razzamatazz and hyberbole, and simplistic focus on glamorous species. When the Foundation became involved in a nationwide fund-raising pledge day aimed at purchasing land for expansion of the Addo Elephant National Park, there was a howl of protest from some leading conservationists, who felt REF was employing dubious methods not appropriate for a wildlife organisation. But the pledge campaign was undertaken with the best intentions and the outcome was more than half a million rand raised, which amount was matched by the South African government and the Southern African Nature Foundation, making possible purchase of more than 1 600 additional hectares of valley bushveld and extending the Addo park by a considerable degree.

In a world where wild country is ever shrinking, and overcrowded on its borders by human beings, one must bear in mind that it is not only the elephants that benefit by expansion of that

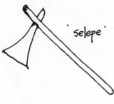

`selepe`

park, or for that matter black rhino; all the inhabitants of the reserve are more secure. It was sad to find ourselves facing opposition on the grounds that South Africa's conservation areas did not need additional land, and that more money was instead needed to increase the salaries of game rangers and for other essentials required in effective park management. That reasoning seemed to border on the ridiculous. So little land is in public ownership in South Africa that any attempt to acquire areas designated irrevocably for conservation must be regarded as a high priority.

By virtue of concentrating on the needs of only two kinds of animals, the Foundation has been able to hone in on specific targets and has had an impressive short history. We do not for a moment deny the importance of conserving broader biological diversity, of course. In fact, we even claim spin-off benefits in that regard. Safeguarding diversity, like safeguarding large animals, can be easier when conserved areas are large. But our argument has always been the same: that we recognize the rational utilisation of a resource.

South Africa is the only country in Africa or the world where sportsmen have in recent years been able to take free-ranging white rhino as a trophy. The by-products of elephant culling operations have provided considerable support to the national parks systems of both Zimbabwe and South Africa. And rural communities living adjacent to elephants in Zimbabwe, as a result of seeing financial benefits from conservation, have come to regard elephants as an asset and a resource, instead of as nothing more than a nuisance. If we are able to develop effective ways of taking care of rhinos and elephants, some of the other aspects of wildlife management will take care of themselves. The slogan, "To hell with the rhino plant a tree" (lately fashionable in knocking large mammal conservation) is designed to underscore the troubles of poverty-stricken people surrounding many parks. But there's nothing contradictory about planting trees *and* conserving rhino.

One should really judge REF by its track record, from the icy waters of the Namibian Skeleton Coast across to the tropical dune forests of Maputaland. The Foundation has been at the forefront of providing equipment and support for rhino and elephant work, and for assisting the game rangers forever expected to guard Africa's heritage. In the brief period from its inception until early 1990, REF had already spent more than R400 000 on rhino and elephant projects chiefly anti-poaching work, translocations, and surveys. Some of the expenditures were decidedly offbeat, the kinds of things government agencies couldn't find funds for in time to address the problems. Consider, for example,

the October 1989 helicopter charter for capture
of black rhino severely threatened by poachers
in the western Caprivi, or the July 1989 alloca-
tion of funds to the Namibian Directorate of
Nature Conservation for purchase of mobile
water pumps for the people of Huab, whose
water supply was regularly being damaged by
elephants.

A symposium organised by REF in 1988 led
directly to a resolution calling upon government
to establish a special endangered species protection unit in the South African Police and called
for much more severe jail sentences and fines
 for people dealing illegally in rhino horn and
ivory. At this writing at last the fines for poaching these animals or dealing in these products
have risen enough to constitute something of a
deterrent. While you need a lot more than just
deterrents in dealing with organised crime,
increased penalties have nevertheless gone a
long way towards enhancing the status of these
two species.

The REF, together with Marie Bruyns and
Richard Beynon of Facet Films, and with support
from the SABC, the National and Natal Parks
Boards, and Ted Reilly of Mkhayi Nature
Reserve, produced an important one-hour docu-
mentary about the ivory trade. *Genesis: The
Resurrection of the African Elephant* examines

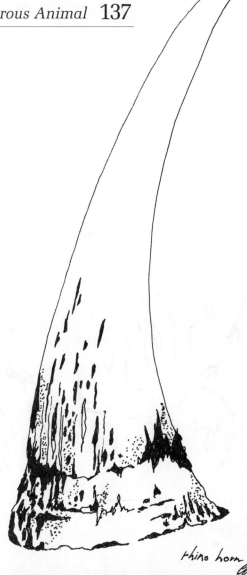

rhino horn

how southern Africa is affected by the international trade ban and attempts to put forward solutions to the problem. Although the elephant in southern Africa is not in immediate danger of extinction, it is worth noting that an illegal ivory trans-shipment system still operates within South Africa. While we have low levels of poaching within this country, the sophisticated, well institutionalised infrastructure has loopholes that have been exploited by dealers in rhino horn and ivory, to their great profit.

At the request of the KwaZulu Bureau of Natural Resources, and funded by Richards Bay Mining Company, REF assisted in black rhino surveys at Ndumu, and in capture and translocation of ten black rhino from the eastern side of Ndumu to the Kruger National Park. Various items have been supplied to the anti-poaching units of both Etosha National Park in Namibia and Operation Stronghold in Zimbabwe; both these black rhino areas have received ongoing REF support over a number of years. And surveillance equipment has been supplied to anti-poaching organisations to assist authorities in combatting declines of both black and white rhino.

Some R33 000 has been contributed by REF towards translocating young elephants from the Kruger Park culling programme to Itala Game Reserve in Natal, and the Foundation helped

Square-lipped (white) rhinoceros.

finance an isotope project at the University of
Cape Town designed to help identify individual
pieces of ivory as to their provenance. REF has
committed further funding to a similar project for
identifying rhino horn. We sponsored a work-
shop about the role of the private sector in future
black rhino conservation, and black rhino have
also been the focus of discussions with the
Department of Wildlife and National Parks in
Botswana. These are but a sampling of REF's projects, and it is clear that they cross the boundaries
of several countries, and of government and non-
governmental organisations. We have also helped
develop a coordinating group of key people in
several of these bodies to direct funds and mini-
mise duplication in the various projects across
southern Africa.

The ultimate success of REF will lie in its role as
a small working group that can provide support
at critical times when agency budgets have
already been allocated, as South Africa's econo-
my faces the increasing demands of the emerging
political situation. The amount of public money
available for conservation will decline, propor-
tionally, and I think it will be incumbent upon all
in the non-governmental conservation movement
to be working in accord as the political mistakes
of the past forty years begin to be redressed, and
urgent human needs and aspirations overshadow
wildlife issues. There is nothing glamorous about

this process. But neither is there any reason for
rhinos and elephants to have to be the victims
one more time.

Epilogue
What Does an Elephant Mean?

Time was when elephants meant adventure, sport, wealth. With the arrival of the first white people on the shores of South Africa, the decline of the African elephant began. For three hundred years the elephant and many other large species of game were systematically decimated. By the beginning of the nineteenth century, the elephant had fallen right back to the upper reaches of the Zambezi and Chobe rivers. Those that remain today in the Cape are only to be found in the Knysna forest – sadly, those animals appear doomed – and in the Addo National Elephant Park, where there are about 150. They are the only viable remnant of the magnificent herds that roamed the forest regions of the Cape of Good Hope. Space is limited in this park, despite a recent addition to it, and culling seems likely to be needed. I still hold out the hope that it may prove possible to relocate young Addo elephant into the Knysna forest.

In the Tembe Elephant Reserve of northern Maputaland, adjoining Mozambique, and in the Kruger National Park are elephants that would probably have been wiped out but for the tracklessness and plagues of fever of Mozambique.

When the twentieth century began, the Transvaal had seen wholesale destruction of elephants by ivory hunters, sportsmen, and settlers. A remnant population in the Kruger Park area survived because malaria kept men at bay, and built up again because healthy elephant populations in Mozambique contributed to it. The western and northern Transvaal saw the total destruction of elephants right to the banks of the Limpopo River. When Jacobs and Selous and the others hunted in those regions, the elephants were retreating into what are now Zimbabwe and Botswana.

Today, under very careful management, there are around eight thousand elephants in the Kruger National park. Young elephants captured during culling programmes there have been reintroduced in the Pilanesberg National Park of Bophuthatswana, bringing elephants back close to the Transvaal heartland. Two females of their number arrived in Pilanesberg via a highly circuitous route. They were born in the Kruger National Park, spent time in the United States, were then taken to Kenya where they were refused entry, and finally brought as young adults to join the group of much younger animals which were being established in Bophuthatswana.

Despite having come under considerable pressure from hunters during the nineteenth century, when vast amounts of ivory came out of what is now Botswana, that country today has some 60 000 elephants. Zimbabwe has a similar number and has, like South Africa, conducted culling programmes for many years. The elephants of Namibia also suffered hunting pressure, although nowhere near as severely as elsewhere in southern Africa, probably because there were never the same densities of elephants there in the first place. Today the Etosha National Park has some 2 500 animals, and small pockets of elephants are to be found in Bushmanland and Caprivi, besides the famous desert-dwelling elephants of the

Kaokoveld. For most people then, in South Africa and Namibia and Zimbabwe, elephants mean national parks. People go to parks for many reasons, but seeing elephants is a prime one. The people need the parks, the elephants need the parks, and the parks need the elephants.

Botswana, by contrast, has two distinct populations of elephants, neither confined to a park. The large northern group inhabits the Okavango Delta, Moremi Game Reserve and Chobe National Park, extending up to the Linyanti swamp and across to the Zimbabwe border. And a relic population of some 600 elephant is to be found in the north-eastern Tuli Block, in an enclave of privately owned game sanctuaries. In many countries where the majority of elephants do not live in designated conservation areas, the animals continue to be viewed locally as prey: a menace to farmers; a source of revenue through guided clients and professional hunting operations; and an ivory supply to be poached as and when possible. Botswana discontinued licensed hunting of elephants in 1983, pending development of a national plan for management of the animals. How legal, licensed hunting will fare in other countries in the wake of the 1989 CITES ban on international traffic in elephant products remains to be seen. But probably there will continue to be places where elephants mean a pinnacle of achievement for sport hunters.

In the end, perhaps it doesn't matter *why* one gets caught up with elephants. They are bound to mean different things to different people. Some may venerate ivory as beautiful, valuable, a kind of living gemstone, warm and textured by comparison with the cool gleam of a diamond or emerald, and they may want to wear it or display carved ivory pieces – investments. It is of course no sin merely to enjoy or admire ivory. The sin lies in forgetting that ivory means elephants.

I'm not sure I can speak to the question of elephant penis lampstands, or elephant foot stools

rolling in a muddy waterhole.
Savuti

with polished toenails. Yes, they are tasteless and absurd, but how different are they in the end from a zebra skin rug or an impala horn bottle opener – or, for that matter, an ivory bangle? Is it better to think about elephants sometimes because you have an elephant foot stool, or not to think about elephants at all? Toenails. Seeing these brings to mind a near-term foetus I once saw during a Kruger Park cull. Any foetuses found in culled cows were being recorded for a population dynamics study. I will never forget the perfect silver-grey toenails of the baby elephant, dead before its time for the greater good of science and the overall park elephant population.

Then there are people for whom the elephant has profound totemic significance, notably among the Zulus and Swazis. In launching the Rhino and Elephant Foundation, KwaZulu Chief Minister Mangosuthu G. Buthelezi noted that the elephant is the central figure on the KwaZulu coat of arms, where it represents strength and intelligence. Zulu kings are praised by being called *Indlovu*, and the king's mother is known as *Ndlovukazi*, the Great She Elephant. Aside from such royal significance, the elephant as a clan totem is a crucial symbol of identity, power, connectedness in the world, binding thousands of people. It is much more than merely a surname.

White people have symbolic moments too. Consider, for example, the definite statement involved in carrying an elephant hide briefcase. It may have been made in Korea or Hong Kong, right alongside cases of other exotic leathers and prime split cow hide, but it doesn't send the same signal as the rest of them. An elephant hide briefcase says: "I love Africa, I want to carry it with me, and I want everyone to know these things." An elephant hair bracelet once said, "I have killed an elephant," but today its message has become less specific: "I identify with big game and wild places." That message remains clear even when some or all of the bracelet is made of gold wire, and whether the wearer is clad in khakis or a Dior tie.

A central element of why these animals have captured our minds is of course their sheer size. The elephant dwarfs us, reminds us we are fragile, even as we impinge upon its numbers and its dignity. Yet we have begun to realize the opportunity that elephants represent: conservation of elephants means conservation of many other creatures and their habitats, because of the extent of areas required to sustain such big animals. The CITES ban on trade in elephant products has its detractors. But, disagreement among the parties notwithstanding, in a real sense that decision by the international wildlife community has focused the world's attention crisply at last. The elephant today embodies wild Africa as never before.

And so it should be, dear Elephant, Sir.

Bull resting against a camelthorn three

Postscript:
Clive Walker
the Man

Clive Walker is the owner of an extremely winning personality. He is genial, quiet about his accomplishments, and thoroughly committed to his ideals.

As many who know him will confirm, his public persona is much like his private one; there are no skeletons in the closet because he faces life square on, and that means acknowledging your error when you are wrong. These essays reflect this. As experience schooled him, he absorbed its lessons and altered his course accordingly.

There are a few things the essays do not reflect, however, which warrant mention. Clive did not become the personification of conservation in South Africa by being born into a wealthy family where he could indulge in unfettered idealism. His Scottish paternal grandfather came to South Africa during the Anglo-Boer War with the 41st Welsh Regiment and was involved in the siege of Kimberley. Demobilised in Johannesburg, Charles Arthur Walker opened a paint and remodelling business that was later taken over by Clive's father. Clive was born in Mayfair in 1936 but his father died in 1944, and times were tough for the family. Although trained as a dental nurse, his mother had to assume control of the business to support her two boys. She ran it until 1980.

Clive did not become a pivotal figure in wilderness trailing and rhino and elephant work through formal training as a naturalist or wildlife manager, either. After schooling at Jeppe preparatory school, Treverton, and St. Andrew's in Bloemfontein, he was planning to embark on a career in art despite his interest in

wild places; occasional hunting forays and wildlife photography trips had to satisfy this interest. But by chance he stumbled upon an offer of work as a ranger in Botswana, in the bad old days when no one enquired how much prospective game wardens actually knew about managing game. He is thus self-taught in the ways of the wild, although, characteristically, his habit is to credit those who guided his thinking – Hans Bufe, Don Richards, Ian Player and others.

Then, as now, being a game ranger paid abysmally low wages, and he gave it up after marrying Conita, to resume an art career in Johannesburg while she kept bread on the table as an airline stewardess. But just as his artistic endeavours were beginning to bear fruit, he encountered the inspiration of wilderness trails. Together he and Conita worked to build up Educational Wildlife Expeditions, a trailing organisation that remains important today. "Together" is the operative word. In every segment of Clive's multifaceted work, Conita has stood squarely beside him, unassuming to a fault, steadily and efficiently contributing her considerable talents and energy to supporting his ventures.

If Clive's frequent absences in the bush complicated Conita's task of raising their two now adult boys, Renning and Anton, one heard no complaint. The involvement with wild places re-

Black rhinoceros at speed.
tail curved over back
CW.

warded the boys with an education broader than any school could offer, and the growing conservation commitment of both their parents made its mark as well. Theirs was no ordinary suburban childhood.

Meanwhile, exhibiting art had led Clive to the United States, where the idea of using paintings to raise money for wildlife settled over him and in due course resulted in his founding the Endangered Wildlife Trust. It was through the Trust that he achieved national prominence as a wildlife advocate; and, like it or not, he has remained highly visible because he proved so good at the job.

He also began to publish. In 1974 he and Don Richards co-authored *Walk through the Wilderness*, a kind of trailist's companion, aimed at enhancing environmental awareness. His well-known *Signs of the Wild* (1981) was in its seventh reprint edition at this writing, and has also been issued in Afrikaans and used as a textbook for professional hunting licence candidates. Later came *Twilight of the Giants*, about elephants in Namibia, Botswana, and Tongaland; collaboration with Anthony Hall-Martin and Hans Grobler on *Predators of Southern Africa*; with Hall-Martin and J. du P. (Koos) Bothma on *Kaokoveld: The Last Wilderness*; and with photographer Herman Potgieter on *Okavango from the Air*.

Most recently he published *Savuti: The vanishing river*.

Another aspect of Clive's life scarcely explored in the current volume is his art. Conservation followers in South Africa are familiar with his work because quantities of it have adorned magazine covers and been sold as fund-raisers. It is clear enough that had he not spent years concentrating more on wildlife than on art, he could have been an artist of considerably greater renown than he is. His first London exhibition (1974) sold out completely. But it suited him to paint for conservation. Paintings helped him raise money for wildlife work. Had he pocketed more of the earnings from his art, Clive could have been a wealthy man. Instead, he still paints in a studio built at his modest Edenvale home (by his mother's construction company) with the eight hundred rand generated by his first Pretoria exhibition of paintings in 1970.

From time to time he has stood accused of "making money out of wildlife". Most of the manufacturers of buffalo hide handbags and springbuck rugs have made a good deal more money than Clive Walker ever has; it's just that they have not been in the public eye as he has. His high profile seems to have made some people think he has unlimited resources, but the truth is that he had depressingly meagre earnings, without pension or medical aid, even when he was almost fifty years old – because he believed in what he was doing.

White rhino

I was among those dismayed in early 1985 to learn that Clive planned to step down from executive directorship of the Endangered Wildlife Trust. Frankly, I didn't believe him when he said he needed to give fuller attention to other things, and neither did I believe his insistence that Dr. John Ledger was going to be an outstanding chief for EWT. But I've been wrong before. John quickly and dramatically expanded the scope of the Trust's work and influence, and Clive moved on the devote himself to the Lapalala reserve and development of its wilderness school, which opened in October the same year.

Then Clive and several wildlife colleagues startled the conservation community with the launching of the Rhino and Elephant Foundation. Why another organisation? Was it justified? That body has had impressive enough achievements in its few years of existence to produce confidence that it was justified. And as regards why it came into being, these essays in part answer that question. Elephants speak to Clive Walker, and he could not bear to watch their decline without taking action designed to help them.

SALLY ANTROBUS

July, 1991

ISBN 1 86812 423 1

First edition, first impression 1992
Published by
Southern Book Publishers (Pty) Ltd
PO Box 3103, Halfway House, 1685

Cover design by Loretta Steyn
Illustrations by Clive Walker
Photograph of the author and his wife on the back flap of the
dustjacket courtesy Andrazj Sawa
Set in 10 on 12pt Melior
by Unifoto Cape Town
Printed and bound by Creda Press Cape Town